Child Health and Well-being 0–6 Years

Niamh Gaine

BORU PRESS

Boru Press Ltd.
The Farmyard
Birdhill
Co. Tipperary
www.borupress.ie

© Niamh Gaines 2021 Reprinted 2022
ISBN 978-1-8384134-7-7

Design by Sarah McCoy
Print origination by Carole Lynch
Illustrations by Andriy Yankovskyy
Printed by Grafo, S.A. (Spain)

The paper used in this book is made from wood pulp of managed forests. For every tree felled, at least one tree is planted, thereby renewing natural resources.

All rights reserved. No part of this publication may be copied, reproduced or transmitted in any form or by any means without written permission of the publishers or else under the terms of any licence permitting limited copyright issued by the Irish Copyright Licensing Agency.

A CIP catalogue record for this book is available from the British Library. For permission to reproduce photographs and artworks, the author and publisher gratefully acknowledge the following:

© Alamy: 80, 131 © Department of Health: 153, 156 © National Poisons Information Centre: 58 © iStock: 67 © Safefood EU: 47 © Shutterstock: 9, 16, 18, 31, 32, 34, 40, 82, 87, 93, 98,112, 114, 116, 117, 119, 120, 124, 126, 127, 128, 129, 130, 134, 142, 149, 150, 153, 154, 166, 171, 175, 176, 177, 178.

The author and publisher have made every effort to trace all copyright holders, but if any has been inadvertently overlooked we would be pleased to make the necessary arrangement at the first opportunity.

Boru Press is an independent publisher and is not associated with any education and training board.

Contents

Acknowledgments — v
Siolta and *Aistear*: An Introduction — 1

Section 1 • Safeguarding Children — 7
1 Safeguarding — 8

Section 2 • Child Well-being — 15
2 Well-being — 16
3 Transitions — 28

Section 3 • Creating a Positive Early Learning and Care Environment — 37
4 Creating an Enriching ELC Environment — 38
5 Hygiene — 43
6 A Safe Environment — 52
7 Record Keeping and Staffing — 69

Section 4 • Personal Care — 73
8 Physical Care Routines — 74

Section 5 • Childhood Illness — 95
9 Childhood Illnesses — 96
10 Childhood Illness in the ELC Setting — 106
11 Infections and Chronic Conditions — 123

Section 6 • Nutrition — 139

12 Nutrition for Babies — 140
13 Nutrition for Toddlers and Young Children — 152

Section 7 • Physical Activity — 169

14 Active Play and Physical Exercise — 170

GLOSSARY — 181

REFERENCES — 183

APPENDICES — 187

USEFUL WEBSITES — 192

INDEX — 194

Acknowledgments

First and foremost, thank you to all my students throughout the years; this book has been shaped by you all.

To my colleagues in Cork ETB and Cork College of Commerce for their support, advice and friendship.

Thanks to my parents Liz and John for always encouraging me to keep studying and learning and to Carol, Seán, Donal and Elaine for the coffee!

Thanks to Eamonn and Bill for reading early drafts and for their suggestions for improvements.

Finally, thank you to Marion, Anna and all the team in Boru Press for their ongoing support, patience and encouragement. The dream team!

Dedication:

Dedicated with love to my nephew Harry Costello

Síolta and *Aistear*: An Introduction

Síolta

Síolta: The National Quality Framework for Early Childhood Education (Department of Education and Skills – DES, 2017) outlines the principles and underlying standards required for a quality ECCE setting. *Síolta* is designed to be used in all services for children from birth to six years, including childminding services, ELC settings and the infant classes in primary school. *Síolta* outlines 16 standards, which are aims that services must meet. Each standard is broken down into components, which provide guidance to enable settings to meet the standards. This book references the following *Síolta* standards:

STANDARD 2: ENVIRONMENTS

Enriching environments both indoor and outdoor (including materials and equipment) are well maintained, safe, available, accessible, adaptable, developmentally appropriate and offer a variety of challenging and stimulating experiences.

STANDARD 3: PARENTS AND FAMILIES

Valuing and involving parents and families requires a proactive partnership approach evidenced by a range of clearly stated, accessible and implemented processes, policies and procedures

STANDARD 9: HEALTH AND WELFARE

Promoting the health and welfare of the child requires protection from harm, provision of nutritious food and appropriate opportunities for rest and secure relationships characterised by trust and respect.

STANDARD 11: PROFESSIONAL PRACTICE

Practising in a professional manner requires that individuals have skills, knowledge, values and attitudes appropriate to their role and responsibility within the setting. In addition, it requires regular reflection upon practice and engagement in supported, ongoing professional development.

STANDARD 13: TRANSITIONS

Ensuring continuity of experiences for children requires policies, procedures and practice that promote sensitive management of transitions, consistency in key relationships, liaison within and between settings, the keeping and transfer of relevant information (with parental consent), and the close involvement of parents and, where appropriate, relevant professionals.

STANDARD 15: LEGISLATION AND REGULATION

Being compliant requires that all relevant regulations and legislative requirements are met or exceeded.

STANDARD 16: COMMUNITY INVOLVEMENT

Promoting community involvement requires the establishment of networks and connections evidenced by policies, procedures and actions which extend and support all adults' and children's engagement with the wider community.

(Source: https://siolta.ie/media/pdfs/siolta-manual-2017.pdf)

Aistear

Aistear is the curriculum framework for all children from birth to six years. Like *Síolta*, *Aistear* is designed to be used in a range of settings including childminding settings, sessional services, full- and part-time day care settings, infant classes in primary schools and children's own homes. *Aistear* aims to help children to grow and develop as confident and competent learners and is based around four themes, each with four aims and 24 learning goals. The four themes of *Aistear* are: Well-being; Identity and Belonging; Communication; and Exploring and Thinking. This book pays special attention to the theme of Well-being but elements of the theme of Exploring and Thinking also come into play.

Aims and Learning Goals for Well-being

	WELL-BEING
Aims	**Learning goals**
Aim 1 Children will be strong psychologically and socially.	In partnership with the adult, children will 1. make strong attachments and develop warm and supportive relationships with family, peers and adults in out-of-home settings and in their community 2. be aware of and name their own feelings, and understand that others may have different feelings 3. handle transitions and changes well 4. be confident and self-reliant 5. respect themselves, others and the environment 6. make decisions and choices about their own learning and development.
Aim 2 Children will be as healthy and fit as they can be.	In partnership with the adult, children will 1. gain increasing control and co-ordination of body movements 2. be aware of their bodies, their bodily functions and their changing abilities 3. discover, explore and refine gross and fine motor skills 4. use self-help skills in caring for their own bodies 5. show good judgment when taking risks 6. make healthy choices and demonstrate positive attitudes to nutrition, hygiene, exercise and routine.

WELL-BEING	
Aims	**Learning goals**
Aim 3 Children will be creative and spiritual.	In partnership with the adult, children will 1. express themselves creatively and experience the arts 2. express themselves through a variety of types of play 3. develop and nurture their sense of wonder and awe 4. become reflective and think flexibly 5. care for the environment 6. understand that others may have beliefs and values different to their own.
Aim 4 Children will have positive outlooks on learning and on life.	In partnership with the adult, children will 1. show increasing independence and be able to make choices and decisions 2. demonstrate a sense of mastery and belief in their own abilities and display learning dispositions, such as determination and perseverance 3. think positively, take learning risks and become resilient and resourceful when things go wrong 4. motivate themselves and welcome and seek challenge 5. respect life, their own and others, and know that life has a meaning and purpose 6. be active citizens.

(Source: https://www.curriculumonline.ie/getmedia/d9604c81-38fc-4660-b592-effb7f70821d/WellBeing_EN.pdf)

Aims and Learning Goals for Exploring and Thinking

EXPLORING AND THINKING	
Aims	**Learning goals**
Aim 1 Children will learn about and make sense of the world around them.	In partnership with the adult, children will 1. engage, explore and experiment in their environment and use new physical skills including skills to manipulate objects and materials 2. demonstrate a growing understanding of themselves and others in their community 3. develop an understanding of change as part of their lives 4. learn about the natural environment and its features, materials, animals and plants, and their own responsibility as carers 5. develop a sense of time, shape, space and place 6. come to understand concepts such as matching, comparing, ordering, sorting, size, weight, height, length, capacity and money in an enjoyable and meaningful way.
Aim 2 Children will develop and use skills and strategies for observing, questioning, investigating, understanding, negotiating and problem solving and come to see themselves as explorers and thinkers.	In partnership with the adult, children will 1. recognise patterns and make connections and associations between new learning and what they already know 2. gather and use information from different sources using their increasing cognitive, physical and social skills 3. use their experience and information to explore and develop working theories about how the world works and think about how and why they learn things 4. demonstrate their ability to reason, negotiate and think logically 5. collaborate with others to share interests and to solve problems confidently 6. use their creativity and imagination to think of new ways to solve problems.

EXPLORING AND THINKING	
Aims	**Learning goals**
Aim 3 Children will explore ways to represent ideas, feelings, thoughts, objects and actions through symbols.	In partnership with the adult, children will 1. make marks and use drawing, painting and model-making to record objects, events and ideas 2. become familiar with and associate symbols (pictures, numbers, letters and words) with the things they represent 3. build awareness of the variety of symbols (pictures, print, numbers) used to communicate, and use these in an enjoyable and meaningful way leading to early reading and writing 4. express feelings, thoughts and ideas through improvising, moving, playing, talking, writing, story-telling, music and art 5. use letters, words, sentences, numbers, signs, pictures, colour and shapes to give and record information, to describe and to make sense of their own and others' experiences 6. use books and ICT (software and the internet) for enjoyment and as a source of information.
Aim 4 Children will have positive attitudes towards learning and develop dispositions like curiosity, playfulness, perseverance, confidence, resourcefulness and risk-taking.	In partnership with the adult, children will 1. demonstrate growing confidence in being able to do things for themselves 2. address challenges and cope with frustrations 3. make decisions and take increasing responsibility for their own learning 4. feel confident that their ideas, thoughts and questions will be listened to and taken seriously 5. develop higher-order thinking skills such as problem-solving, predicting, analysing, questioning and justifying 6. act on their curiosity, take risks and be open to new ideas and uncertainty

(Source: https://www.curriculumonline.ie/Early-Childhood/Principles-and-Themes/)

Section 1

Safeguarding Children

Safeguarding

After reading this chapter you will:
- be able to explain the concept of safeguarding
- understand the legal responsibilities of an ELC (Early Learning and Care) practitioner to safeguard children.

Key Terms

Harm: The Children First Act 2015 defines harm as assault, ill-treatment or neglect of the child which seriously affects or is likely to seriously affect the child's health, development or welfare. Any sexual abuse of the child is classified as harm under the 2015 Act.

Mandated person: As listed in the Children First Act 2015, a mandated person has legal responsibilities to report child protection concerns above a defined threshold to Tusla (the Child and Family Agency responsible for improving well-being and outcomes for children). ELC practitioners are mandated persons.

Safeguarding: the principles and procedures to be observed in an ELC setting to keep children safe from harm.

What is Safeguarding?

'Safeguarding' is a term that describes the principles and procedures to be observed in an ELC setting to keep children safe from harm. A Child Safeguarding Statement is a written statement that specifies the service being provided by the ELC setting and the principles and procedures to be observed in order to ensure, as far as practicable, that children attending the ELC setting are safe from harm. It should set out any potential risk of harm to children that have been identified in the risk assessment, and procedures in place to reduce the identified risks, as specified in Section 11 (3) of the Children First Act 2015. All ELC settings are required to have a safeguarding statement, and the Department of Children, Equality, Disability, Integration and Youth (DCEDIY) has published a guidelines document to support ELC settings in developing this. All staff must be familiar with the contents of the safeguarding statement.

A Child Safeguarding Statement will contain:

1. an assessment of the potential for harm occurring to a child while attending the ELC setting or participating in activities organised by the ELC setting
2. details about the setting, including the name of the setting and the activities it provides
3. the principles and the procedures observed in the setting in order to keep children safe.

Look it up

Source and read the Child Safeguarding Statement and the Child Protection and Welfare Reporting Procedure that are followed in your placement setting.

Legislation

The Children First Act was enacted in 2015. This act:

* raises awareness of child abuse and neglect
* provides for mandatory reporting by key professionals (including ELC practitioners)
* improves child safeguarding arrangements in organisations that provide services to children

* provides for cooperation and information sharing between agencies when Tusla is undertaking a child protection assessment.

The legislation is supported by *Children First: National Guidance for the Protection and Welfare of Children* (DCYA, 2017). This resource aims to support ELC settings and staff in adhering to the 2015 legislation.

Online course

Tusla's 'Introduction to Children First' e-learning programme provides the most up-to-date training on the Children First Act 2015. You will be required to complete this before you begin your Professional Placement.

MANDATED REPORTING

A mandated person has legal responsibilities for the safeguarding of children under the Children First Act 2015. Mandated persons have two responsibilities:

1. to report the harm of children above a defined threshold to Tusla
2. to assist Tusla, if requested, in assessing a concern that has been the subject of a mandated report.

ELC practitioners are mandated persons and **so have the legal responsibility to report any knowledge, belief, or reasonable suspicion that a child has been harmed, is being harmed or is at risk of being harmed**.

WHAT IS MEANT BY 'HARM'?

The Children First Act 2015 defines harm in two ways:

1. assault, ill-treatment, or neglect of the child that seriously affects or is likely to seriously affect the child's health, development or welfare
2. sexual abuse of the child.

The threshold of harm (the point at which you must report to Tusla under the Children First Act 2015) is reached when you know, believe or have reasonable grounds to suspect that:

* a child's needs have been neglected, are being neglected, or are at risk of being neglected to the point where the child's health, development or welfare have been or are being seriously affected, or are likely to be seriously affected

OR

* a child has been, is being or is at risk of being ill-treated to the point where the child's health, development or welfare have been or are being seriously affected, or are likely to be seriously affected

OR

* a child has been, is being or is at risk of being assaulted, and that as a result the child's health, development or welfare have been or are being seriously affected, or are likely to be seriously affected

OR

* a child has been, is being or is at risk of being sexually abused.

HOW DO I KNOW IF A CHILD HAS BEEN, IS BEING OR IS AT RISK OF BEING HARMED?

The following should be taken as **reasonable grounds for concern** which indicate a child has been, is being or is at risk of being harmed:

* an injury or behaviour that is consistent with abuse and is unlikely to have been caused in any other way
* any concerns about potential sexual abuse
* consistent signs that the child is suffering from emotional or physical neglect
* a child saying or otherwise indicating that they have been abused
* an admission or indication by an adult or child of an alleged abuse they committed
* a statement from a person who saw the child being abused.

How do I make a report?

The Tusla 'Child Protection and Welfare Report Form' is available on the Tusla website and can be completed in hard copy or through the secure web portal: https://www.tusla.ie/children-first/web-portal/. You can also make a report over the phone.

The Rights of Children and their Families

The Irish Constitution (*Bunreacht na hÉireann*) give rights to both children (Article 42A) and their families (Article 41). You will learn more about these rights over the duration of your course.

In the context of safeguarding children, Article 42A places a responsibility on us all to act in the *best interest of the child*. This means that we have a responsibility and duty of care to support and protect the children in our care and to put their interests and welfare above everything else.

Article 41 gives special consideration to the rights of the family. The family is the first educator of the child and so has the right to be involved in all aspects of their child's life and education. If you are making a mandated report, it is best practice to tell parents/guardians that you are doing so, unless you believe that telling the parents/guardians will put the child at further risk of harm. In the case of an emergency, and if the duty social worker is unavailable, you should contact An Garda Síochana.

Families have a right to know what is happening in their child's life and cooperation with families is essential for child protection cases. Therefore, you must be sensitive and professional in how you deal with families at all times.

RESPONSIBILITIES OF CONFIDENTIALITY WHEN SAFEGUARDING CHILDREN

Any information in relation to child protection matters must be handled with the strictest confidentiality. You must not share information, even accidentally, that would breach this. However, there are two exceptions to this rule:

1. You must cooperate and share information, in your role as a mandated person, with Tusla and An Garda Síochána.

2. If you are making a report on a child in your setting you must also inform the designated liaison person (DLP). Every ELC setting must have a DLP. As a mandated person you can make a joint report with the DLP.

It may happen that a child directly discloses something to you about harm that they are currently experiencing or that they have experienced. You **cannot** keep any direct disclosures a secret and, as a mandated person, you **must** report to Tusla.

CASE STUDY: SAFEGUARDING RESPONSIBILITIES IN THE ELC SETTING

Natalia works in the Toddler Room of a large ELC setting. Recently, Natalia has started to become a little worried about one of the children in her room. Melissa is 2 and attends five mornings a week. Melissa is a nervous child. She tends to jerk at loud noises in the room and can often seem 'on edge'. She often wears the same clothes for several days in a row, and sometimes there is a musty smell from her clothes. Melissa's mum always seems to be in a hurry at drop-off and collection time. She rarely stops to chat with Natalia or to ask about Melissa's day.

Today Melissa seems very 'off form'. When Natalia was changing Melissa's nappy, she saw an unusual mark in the shape of a handprint on Melissa's tummy. Melissa is very clingy today and cries if Natalia tries to put her down or play with another child.

Questions

1. Are there grounds for reasonable concern in this situation? What are they?
2. What are Natalia's legal responsibilities in this situation?
3. Make a list of the next steps Natalia should take to safeguard Melissa.

SAFEGUARDING WHEN PERFORMING CHILDREN'S PHYSICAL CARE ROUTINES

As an ELC practitioner you will have to assist children in their physical care routines. Supporting children in their physical care routines may include providing support with dressing and undressing (including underwear), changing nappies, helping a child to use the toilet or cleaning private parts of the child's body. You will learn more about physical care routines in Chapter 8. When assisting children in their physical care routines, you must take steps to safeguard children. When changing a child's nappy or assisting them with toileting, it is best practice to have another ELC practitioner in the vicinity if possible, and the other practitioner should be aware that the activity is taking place. Encourage children to be as independent as possible in their physical care, in line with what is developmentally appropriate. Smartphones and tablets should be banned in the nappy changing/toileting area.

Further reading

The Best Interests of the Child (McPartland, 2020) gives a comprehensive overview of the Children First legislation and the responsibilities it places on mandated persons.

Section 2

Child Well-being

Well-being

After reading this chapter you will:

* understand the factors that support the development of children's emotional well-being
* appreciate the importance of the role of the adult and reciprocal warm interactions when working in an ELC setting.

Key Term

Key person: the ELC practitioner responsible for the provision of the lead support, contact and communication for an individual child and their family within the ELC setting.

Aistear Theme of Well-being

The *Aistear* theme of Well-being has four aims:

1. Children will be strong psychologically and socially.
2. Children will be as healthy and fit as they can be.
3. Children will be creative and spiritual.
4. Children will have positive outlooks on learning and on life.

The theme of Well-being takes a broad view of the definition of well-being. It includes not only physical and psychological well-being, but also creative, spiritual and social well-being and intellectual curiosity. It involves wellness in the full sense of the word.

PSYCHOLOGICAL AND SOCIAL WELL-BEING

Psychological and social well-being are linked. In an ELC setting, this involves developing attachment relationships and helping children to deal with their emotions and feelings and to handle transitions in their lives, including being apart from their parents, moving between rooms in the setting and moving from the setting to primary school.

PHYSICAL WELL-BEING

Physical well-being is covered in Aim 2: 'Children will be as healthy and fit as they can be' (National Council for Curriculum and Assessment – NCCA, 2009, p. 17). Physical well-being includes the development of gross and fine motor skills and self-care skills. ELC settings must help children to develop autonomy and independence and to master such skills as self-feeding, putting on and taking off their own coat, and toilet training.

CREATIVITY AND SPIRITUALITY

Creativity and spirituality refer to encouraging children to explore the arts and the environment around them. Spirituality does not mean that the ELC practitioner must teach the customs and beliefs of a particular religion; rather it involves teaching children a sense of 'wonder and awe' about the world around them and a respect for all beliefs.

INTELLECTUAL CURIOSITY

The final aspect of well-being involves encouraging children to have a sense of curiosity about the world and an interest in learning. Children should be encouraged to engage in active learning and to develop confidence in their own abilities. (See *Síolta and Aistear: An Introduction*, pages 1–2.)

CASE STUDY: WELL-BEING IN ACTION

(Note: The numbers in brackets relate to the relevant sections in *Aistear*'s Well-being theme.)

Sunshine Pre-School meets *Aistear*'s theme of Well-being. The routine is designed to ensure that children have enough time for rest, nutrition and play (2.6). A key person system is in operation, helping children to feel secure in the setting (1.1). The setting has a policy on helping children to handle transitions: when a new child begins in the pre-school their parents can spend time in the setting to help the child feel at ease. Practitioners will also help children through transitions in their lives by talking and listening to them. An end-of-year celebration is held to celebrate the children's transition from the setting to primary school (1.3). Sunshine Pre-School offers a play-based curriculum (3.2). The weekly plan includes time for arts and crafts (3.1) and physical activities, including music and movement (2.1, 2.2). Circle time is held daily to allow children space to discuss their feelings (1.2) and to introduce topics such as self-care skills (2.4), healthy eating (2.6) and keeping children safe (2.5). A mix of child- and adult-directed activities are planned, allowing children time to make choices (4.1, 4.6); and in doing so, the setting enables children to learn to make decisions for themselves and be confident in their own abilities (1.6, 3.4, 4.6). By planning around the theme of Well-being, Sunshine Pre-School prepares children to enter primary school as 'confident, happy and healthy' individuals.

A Framework for Providing for Children's Well-being

Maslow's hierarchy of human needs (Maslow, 1954) can be useful for thinking about how ELC settings and ELC practitioners can provide for children's well-being.

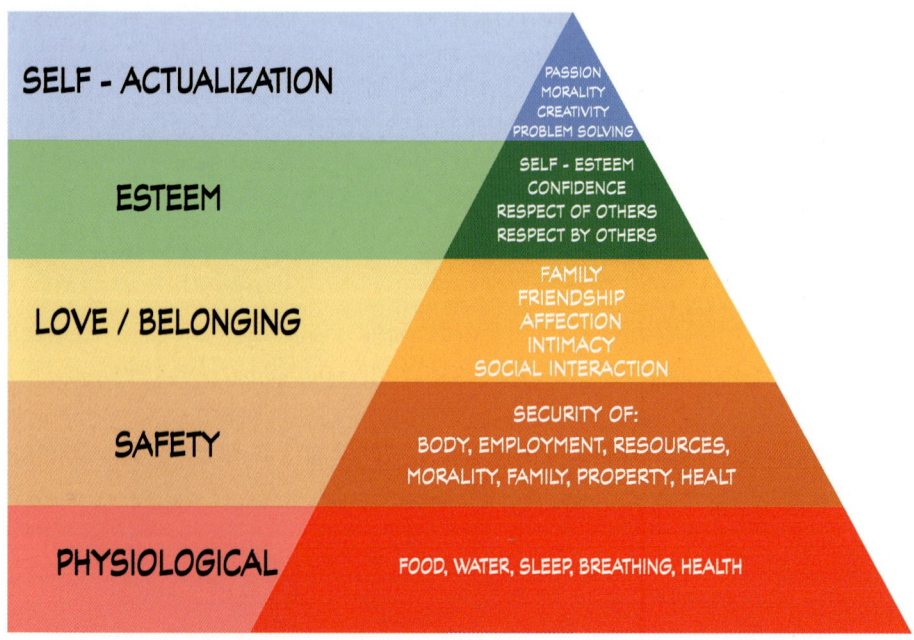

Maslow's hierarchy of needs

PHYSIOLOGICAL NEEDS

The bottom level in Maslow's hierarchy is our physiological, or basic, needs. These are the needs that must be met in order to stay alive. Meeting children's basic needs is the foundation for well-being. Children's basic needs in an ELC setting include those shown in this graphic.

Children need clean water and food to stay alive. Their environment must be clean, hygienic and warm. They need plenty of fresh air and exercise. Children must be stimulated with toys and activities, and they require quiet time for rest and sleep. If all these factors are present, children's basic needs will be met.

SAFETY AND SECURITY

Once our physiological needs are met, our need for safety and security becomes important. We need to be physically safe in our environment (Chapter 6 discusses safety in an ELC setting). We also need to feel emotionally safe, in other words, to have relationships with others and attachment figures. Attachment is discussed in more detail later in this chapter

LOVE AND BELONGING

Once our need for safety and security is met, we need love and belonging. We need to feel loved and that we belong in social groups. Children need to have warm and caring relationships with both adults and other children. The need for love and belonging can be met in an ELC setting by operating a key person system. The key person system is discussed in more detail later in this chapter.

SELF-ESTEEM

Our need for self-esteem refers to our need to feel good about ourselves. This need can be met in an ELC setting by encouraging children based on their efforts, respecting children, listening to the voice of the child and valuing the process over the product in their creative work.

> ### It's the process, not the product!
> The golden rule of working with young children is to always focus on the process and not the product. This means we comment and support the work and play children do and not the end result. When we focus on the process, we build children's curiosity, confidence and self-esteem. (The Curiosity Approach, 2019)

SELF-ACTUALISATION

The final layer in Maslow's hierarchy is our need for self-actualisation. This refers to our need to fulfil our potential and 'be all we can be'. This need can be met by providing a challenging and stimulating ELC curriculum, which makes use of children's funds of knowledge and is based on their emerging interests.

Developing Children's Autonomy

One of the goals of ELC settings is to help children to develop age-appropriate independence and autonomy. Children should be given the freedom to try things for themselves. They should also be given appropriate responsibilities. For example, the pre-school class can be asked to tidy up toys or to help with putting out materials for an activity or at snack time or lunchtime. In developing children's autonomy, we are preparing them for life and giving them the skills they need. This also helps to develop children's self-esteem.

CASE STUDY: ELC IN SAN MINIATO

In 2018, I was lucky enough to be given the opportunity to go on an Early Childhood Ireland study trip to San Miniato in Northern Italy. In San Miniato, the child from birth to 3 years is viewed as a **protagonist of their learning**, which means that the child is viewed as independent and capable. Children have the freedom to move around the setting independently and at their own pace.

In the first setting we visited, I was surprised to be greeted by a group of children, all under the age of 3, who ran to the closed gate to meet us, with no sign of an adult present. The practitioner followed and let us in, and the children ran to various parts of the outside area and on to the next thing that caught their attention. The practitioners explained to us that in San Miniato children are trusted to move as they please. The environment is prepared and designed to be safe and accommodating for all the children, and children have freedom within the limits of the prepared environment. I asked if they were worried that the children would hurt themselves if they were out of sight and was told, 'No. There is nothing to hurt them here and we trust them.' The focus on viewing each child as independent and capable was further reinforced at mealtimes. The children assisted with the tasks of mealtime, pouring water from a glass jug into real glasses and spooning out their pasta for lunch into real bowls, using a large ladle. Throughout, they were supported by the practitioner, who encouraged each child to be independent and capable, and who only intervened if absolutely necessary – and often didn't intervene at all.

The trip to San Miniato made me reflect on the importance of giving children autonomy and freedom within a prepared environment.

Monitoring Children's Well-being and Involvement

Well-being is about children having a positive sense of themselves and others, and a positive disposition to learn. Dr Ferre Laevers, working at Leuven University in Belgium, has developed two scales that can assist ELC practitioners to judge children's well-being and involvement in an activity, as outlined in the following tables.

MEASURING CHILDREN'S WELL-BEING

Well-being	Signs
Level 1: **Extremely low**	The child shows signs of discomfort, such as crying or screaming. They may look dejected, sad, frightened or angry. The child is not responding to the environment, avoids contact and is withdrawn. The child may behave aggressively, hurting themselves or others.
Level 2: **Low**	Posture, facial expression and actions indicate that the child does not feel at ease. However, the signals are not as strong as in level 1, or the discomfort is not expressed the whole time.
Level 3: **Moderate**	The child has a neutral posture. Facial expression and posture show little or no emotion. No signs indicating sadness or pleasure, comfort or discomfort.
Level 4: **High**	The child shows obvious signs of satisfaction (as in level 5). However, these signals are not constantly present with the same intensity.
Level 5: **Extremely high**	The child looks happy and cheerful, and smiles or cries out with pleasure. They may be lively and full of energy. Action can be spontaneous and expressive. The child may talk to themselves, play with sounds, hum and sing. The child appears relaxed and does not show any signs of distress or tension. The child expresses self-confidence and self-assurance.

MEASURING CHILDREN'S INVOLVEMENT

Involvement	Signs
1 **Low activity**	Activity is simple, stereotypic, repetitive and passive. The child seems absent and displays no energy. There is an absence of cognitive demand.
2 **A frequently interrupted activity**	The child is engaged in activity, but half of the observed period includes moments of non-activity, in which the child is not concentrating and stares into space. There may be frequent interruptions in the child's concentration, but their involvement is not enough to return to the activity.
3 **Mainly continuous activity**	The child is busy at an activity, but it is at a routine level and real signs of involvement are missing. Energy is lacking, and concentration is at a routine level. The child can be easily distracted.
4 **Continuous activity with intense moments**	The child's activity has intense moments where they seem involved in the activity. They are not easily distracted.
5 **Sustained intense activity**	The child shows continuous and intense activity, revealing the greatest level of involvement. The child displays concentration, creativity, energy and persistence in their activity. This intensity must be present for almost the full observation period.

The Ferre Laevers scale **should not be used to measure or assess children**. Instead, it is a tool to judge how children are feeling and their level of involvement in an activity. It can assist the ELC practitioners in responding to children's needs.

Attachment Theory

As you will learn in other areas of your course, emotional development is an essential aspect of children's development. This includes the development of emotional security and forming bonds of attachment with others. An attachment is a 'close emotional relationship between two people' (Shaffer, 2005, p. 131). Child development theorists emphasise the importance of close emotional relationships with adults. The child's attachment figures act as a secure base from which the child can explore the world around them.

MULTIPLE ATTACHMENTS

Research indicates that babies and young children make multiple attachments and attach to more than one person (Schaffer and Emerson, 1964; Rutter, 1981). This is true even for very young babies. In 1964, two researchers, Rudolph Schaffer and Peggy Emerson, designed a study to investigate attachments in babies. The results showed that babies experienced multiple attachments and could have distinct bonds of attachment with several people. Children can and do form attachments with many key people in their lives, including their mothers, fathers, grandparents, aunts and uncles, brothers and sisters, and ELC practitioners. Even very small babies have distinct relationships with different people, and the child attaching to many people is a factor in their emotional well-being. In the words of Schaffer, 'love has no limits' (Schaffer, 1977, p. 100).

ATTACHMENT IN ELC SETTINGS

Attachment theory emphasises the importance of children having a secure base to explore the world around them. In ELC settings, the key person will act as a secure base for the child. The key person is someone who is specially assigned to a number of children and who develops a particular relationship with those individual children. This helps children to settle in the setting and lessens any separation anxiety they may feel when leaving their parent/guardian. The role of the key person is essential for providing for children's emotional well-being in ELC settings. The Effective Provision of Pre-school Education (EPPE) project found that children make most progress when cared for by warm staff who respond to their needs. This is also highlighted in *Aistear*, which emphasises the need for a 'reciprocal relationship' between the child and carer.

RECIPROCAL RELATIONSHIPS AND INTERACTIONS

Both *Aistear* (NCCA, 2009) and *Síolta* (DES, 2017) discuss the importance of relationships in ELC settings. *Aistear* states that children 'learn and develop through loving and nurturing relationships with adults and other children' (p. 9). Similarly, *Síolta* states that 'responsive, sensitive and reciprocal relationships, which are consistent over time, are essential to the well-being, learning and development of the young child' (p. 7).

This means that ELC practitioners need to be warm and caring in their relationships with children. Children need to have individual time with the practitioner and to develop relationships with those who care for them. This is sometimes referred to as a 'nurturing pedagogy' (Hayes and Kernan, 2008).

Positive and nurturing interactions in an ELC setting form the basis for everything that happens in the setting. This should be agreed and understood by everyone across the setting. Positive interactions are facilitated by the following factors:

* **Working and spending time down on the child's level:** You need to spend time down on the floor with children, engaging them on their physical level. As adults, we are a lot bigger than children, and this can be intimidating. When we get down to the child's level, we help them to feel secure and respected.

* **Speaking in a warm and nurturing tone of voice:** You should speak calmly and not in a rushed manner. Your tone should be at a slightly higher pitch then it would when speaking to adults. Developmental psychologists and linguists call this 'infant-directed speech'. It has been found to be beneficial for children's language, social and emotional development.

* **Use positive body language with eye contact:** It is estimated that nonverbal communication and body language make up two-thirds of our communication. When working with young children, remember to smile – it goes a long way!

* **Sitting quietly with the child:** Sometimes children just need the adult to sit with them and to be present. Take your lead from the child and judge if this is something they need in the moment.

* **Modelling how to complete a task:** We model a task or action for young children when we show them how to do something. Children love to learn from the adults in their lives.

* **Playing with children when invited in:** Play alongside children, following their lead and the direction of their play.

* **Observing the child and intervening mindfully:** Sometimes the best way to nurture children is to stand back and observe them playing together. In play, children develop social and emotional bonds with each other. You can intervene if needed, for example to give them some knowledge to support their play.

* **Asking open-ended questions of children:** An open-ended question is a broad question, which has no right or wrong answer. For example, 'Why do you think that happened?' Open-ended questions give children the freedom to test their ideas and theories. Don't worry if the child doesn't answer straight away, and be careful not to jump in and answer your own question. Remember: children are still mastering language and may just need more time to respond.

* **Commenting on what the children are doing rather than asking direct questions:** It is important not to bombard the child with questions. If we do this it can put children under pressure. Sometimes it can be better to comment on or describe what the child is doing. For example, 'I can see you are painting a blue pattern.' When we do this, we show the child that we are interested in them and in what they are doing.

* **'Go with the flow' and go where the children take you:** It is important to follow the child's lead. Allow them to dictate the direction of play or the nature of the interaction.

It may seem like the above tips are contradictory – and in fact, they are! Working with children is a complex task and there is no such thing as a 'one size fits all' approach. Think of the above strategies as a paintbox. When we combine all the colours together in different ways, we can create a beautiful picture, but we need different colours for different tasks. Similarly, we combine all of the above interaction strategies when working in ELC settings. Different interaction strategies do different jobs, but when combined, they will help to develop warm and caring relationships with the children.

> Providing for children's wellbeing requires inclusive practice. In 2018 the DCYA published a *Code of Professional Responsibilities and Code of Ethics for Early Years Educators.* It states that ELC practitioners 'respect diversity and ensure that all children and families have their individual, personal, cultural and linguistic identity valued' (2018, p. 5). This means that to support children's wellbeing, ELC practitioners must adopt an inclusive and anti-bias approach to their work. When we show that we value a child's identity we promote them to feel love and a sense of belonging and which helps their self-esteem. You can learn more about how to create an inclusive ELC environment in Chapter 4.

KEY PERSON

A key person approach is used in ELC settings to help children to form secure attachments and build close relationships. The key person will be responsible for the provision of the lead support, contact and communication for a child and their family within the ELC setting.

The key person will:

* be the main point of contact for parents and families when the child starts in the setting and at daily arrival and departure times
* get to know each child's interests, preferences, temperament, ways of communicating (verbal and nonverbal), emotional and physical needs, and will respond to these sensitively
* be aware of the child's language, background and culture, and ensure that these are understood, respected and reflected in the setting
* be a secure base for the child from which they can explore and interact with others
* observe, assessing and recording the child's learning and development, and help to plan new experiences that build on the child's interests and help them to learn and develop in a holistic way
* share important information with parents, for example when the baby, toddler or young child does or says something new, or when they particularly enjoy something
* ease transitions for the child by introducing new experiences and people, and help the child to cope with change.

The key person approach has been found to have benefits for all stakeholders: for babies and young children, for parents and families, for the key person and for the ELC setting (Elfer, Goldschmied and Selleck, 2003). For babies and children, the key person takes care of their needs and helps the child to feel valued and secure away from home. The key person is also essential for helping children to manage transitions. Parents and families can build a relationship with a person in the setting who is familiar with their baby or child, which can help them to feel more secure leaving the child in the setting. The key person will experience the reward of the bond with the child. The setting will benefit from greater staff involvement and the resulting improved quality of care and learning for the child, as well as positive relationships with parents and families.

CASE STUDY: KEY PERSON IN ACTION

Jake is an ELC practitioner in Little Miracles ELC setting. Jake is the key person for three children in the Toddler Room. Every day, Jake greets his key children and their parents. He gets down to the children's level to welcome them to the setting. If any of the parents need to tell Jake anything, they can do so. During the day, Jake is responsible for the physical care of his key children. He accompanies the children to the bathroom and gives assistance if needed or in the case of any toileting accidents. Jake is also responsible for documenting the children's learning using the *Aistear* Learning Record Template. Little Miracles uses an app to communicate with parents. During the day, Jake takes photographs of the children to share with their parents on the app. The parents love getting these photographs, as it keeps them informed of their child's day.

Transitions

After reading this chapter you will:

* be enabled to support children in manging transitions in their lives.

> **Key Term**
>
> **Transition:** the term given to the process of a person moving from one situation to another. It is not considered complete until the person has fully settled in.

A transition is the name given to the process of a person moving from one situation to another and is not considered complete until the person has fully settled in (Graham, 2012). Transitions are complex and multi-layered. They can be:

* **Physical** – requiring children to move from one physical place to another. For example, children moving between rooms in the ELC setting.
* **Emotional** – requiring children to navigate their feelings and emotions. For example, when a new baby is born into a one-child family the older child will undergo an emotional transition from being an only child to being an older sibling.
* **Social** – requiring children to move to a different social circle. For example, when the child starts to attend an ELC setting they will be mixing socially with adults and children with whom they would not have mixed previously.

Transitions can be difficult for children. Whether a transition is physical, emotional or social, they are required to leave one situation behind and adapt to the new one, with all its associated rules, norms and responsibilities. Think about how you felt when you started your college course. Perhaps you felt nervous, anxious, worried, excited or happy. A child may feel all these emotions when they transition from room or setting to another, or even from one activity to another. However, children may not have the language to explain how they feel and why they feel like this. As an ELC practitioner, you must provide a safe, supportive base for young children to negotiate these transitions.

Standard 13 of *Síolta* is all about transitions and discusses the importance of continuity of experience for children during transitions. To do this requires:

> "policies, procedures and practice that promote sensitive management of transitions, consistency in relationships, liaison within and between settings, the keeping and transfer of relevant information (with parental consent), and the close involvement of parents, and where appropriate, relevant professionals (DES, 2017, p. 85)."

The *Aistear Síolta Practice Guide* (www.aistearsiolta.ie) categorises transitions into three groups: daily transitions, regular transitions and major transitions, as outlined in this table:

Daily transitions	Daily arrival in the setting
	Home time
	Moving from one activity to another
	Beginning and ending care routines, e.g. toileting, sleep
	Moving from indoors to outdoors and vice versa
	Tidy-up time
Regular transitions	Moving to a new room in the setting
	Change of key person
	Attending an additional service, e.g. going to speech and language therapy
Major transitions	Moving from home to the ELC setting
	Moving from the ELC setting to primary school
	Moving from one ELC setting to another
	Life transitions, e.g. the arrival of a new baby, moving house, bereavement or relationship break-up

Daily Transitions

Every day the child is in the ELC setting there will be many transitions. Some examples include transitioning from free play to a more structured activity, from an indoor activity to an outdoor activity, and from the setting to home time. Children respond to consistency and structure in their routine. For this reason, the setting should try to minimise the amount of disruption during the day. Staff break times should be staggered so that at least one familiar staff member is always with the children. Similarly, holiday rosters should be managed so that children have familiar staff with them as much as possible. The child should be at the core of how all transitions are managed. Every child will have a different temperament and disposition, and you should always follow the child's lead.

During daily transitions, for example from one activity to another, flexible routines and structures should be put in place to help children to understand that one activity is coming to an end and another is starting. Here are some ideas:

* Display pictures of the daily routine. This can be very useful for providing children with a visual reminder of the daily routine and what comes next.
* Dim the lights or use sand timers as visual cues before a transition.
* Sing songs and recite rhymes to help during a transition. This provides an audio cue to alert children that a transition is about to occur. It can also act as a reminder for the activity that needs to be undertaken, for example singing a 'clean-up' song when it is time to tidy up after a structured activity.
* Use puppets. This can be a non-threatening way to signal and ease children into a transition.

It is most important to be calm and gradual in managing daily transitions. Children should never be rushed or put under pressure to 'move faster'. After all, you wouldn't like it if you were rushed!

ARRIVAL AND DEPARTURE TIME

These important transitions should be warm and focused on the child. Make sure to greet each child individually and on their level. Ask the parents how the child is and how their night was. Give the child a role in arrival or departure, for example some settings will have a 'signing-in' station where children can move their photo from one column to another to indicate if they are 'in' or 'out'.

Regular Transitions

While regular transitions occur less frequently than daily transitions, they can still be unsettling for the child. An example of a regular transition is when children return to the setting after a short break, for example after Christmas or Easter holidays. It can sometimes take children a short while to readjust after having a break from the ELC setting, but before long they will be back in their normal routine.

TRANSITIONS WITHIN THE ELC SETTING FROM ONE ROOM TO ANOTHER

Children who are in full day care will transition from one room to another over their time in the setting. This is often determined by age. For example, a child may transition from the Wobbler room to the Toddler Room at 2 years of age and will then move to the ECCE room the September after they turn 2 years 8 months. This transition should be treated similarly to the child's initial transition in the setting. The key person has a real impact here. Visits to the new room are an excellent way to start this transition. The key person can take the child to the new room and spend some time with them there. If the child settles, then the key person can leave the child for a while and then return the child back to their 'home room'. This should be repeated several times over a period of a few weeks. Some children will take longer to settle than others – this is okay; every child will adapt at their own pace. Never push a child or force a child to stay somewhere they are uncomfortable. Instead, break the visits into smaller chunks and spread them out over a longer period of time. The child will eventually settle in the new room.

Partnership with parents

It is really important to work closely with parents when transitioning the child from one room to another in the ELC setting. They should be informed that the change is coming and be introduced to the staff in the new room before the transition begins.

Major Transitions

TRANSITIONING FROM HOME TO THE ELC SETTING

The first major educational transition in young children's lives is the transition from home to the ELC setting. The ELC setting must be sensitive to children to help them adjust to this transition. The *Aistear*

theme of Identity and Belonging is very useful here. The ELC setting should be warm and caring towards each child and should, like a loving parent, enfold each and every child (Graham, 2012, p. 3).

The foundations for a successful transition from home to the ELC setting begin before a child is even enrolled in the setting. The ELC setting should share information about the setting with parents to help parents to decide if it will be a good fit for their child. A home visit is a great idea to introduce the key person to the child before they begin in the setting. This is really useful, as it means the child's first meeting with the key person is in a place where the child is comfortable. When the child enrols in the setting, the setting should gather information from the parent about the child, such as their likes and dislikes, eating patterns and any special comfort objects. Each ELC setting will have a 'settling in' policy, which parents should be familiar with. Different strategies can be used to help the child to settle in. For example:

* Invite the parent to spend time in the setting with their child.
* Stagger the number of new children who start at one time.
* Have the child attend the setting for shorter days and gradually increase their hours over a period of time.
* The ELC setting and parent should work closely together and follow the lead of the child. Some children will adapt easily to the setting; others will need more support. Never force a child to stay in a situation that they are not comfortable in.

The transition from home to the ELC setting can also be stressful for parents who are worried and want to know if their child is adapting. The ELC setting should share photos and videos of the child with their parents to help with this. Apps like Child Paths, TeachKloud and ClassDojo are useful for this, as the parent can see the photo or video instantly on their phone, which can reassure them.

It is really important to provide the children with reminders of home to help with the transition. This might involve parents sending a comfort

blanket or soother into the setting with the child. These are sometimes referred to as transitional objects. A lot of settings will have a 'family wall'. This is a special part of the setting where photographs of people who are important to the child can be placed. This is very good for helping with children's sense of identity and belonging.

As previously mentioned in this chapter, the role of the key person is essential for a smooth transition to the setting. Sensitive reciprocal relationships with the key person are essential for helping children to manage transitions in their lives.

Inclusive practice

For children who speak English as an additional language (EAL), it is very important to learn some key words in their first, or home, language. It helps the child to feel secure and helps to maintain the link between the ELC setting and home. It also shows the child and family that you value and respect their cultural identity. Never stop a child from speaking in their home language; it is important for their feelings of confidence and security and for thinking about and processing the events of the day (Bruce, Meggitt and Grenier, 2016).

Look it up

Source and read the 'Settling In' policy that is followed in your Professional Practice setting.

TRANSITIONING FROM THE ELC SETTING TO PRIMARY SCHOOL

Research has shown that the transition from the ELC setting to primary school is a very important time in children's lives. A positive experience during this transition has been shown to be associated with positive social, emotional and educational outcomes for children. Because of this, it is really important that parents, ELC practitioners and primary school teachers all work together and with the child to ensure the smoothest transition possible. Some children need special supports during this transition, including children experiencing social and economic disadvantage, children with English as an additional language and children with additional needs. The move to primary school is complex and involves lots of changes for children. Not only are they in a different physical environment, but they also have to negotiate a whole new culture. Schools may have uniforms and rules, whereas the ELC setting will not, and the school routine may be less flexible than the daily or weekly routines in the ELC setting. The move to primary school also involves a change in social status and identity for children. They start to think of themselves as a school child and to figure out who they are in school. We communicate this explicitly to children when we describe the transition as going to 'big school' – the implication being that they are now a 'big child' and not a young child anymore.

HOW CAN ELC PRACTITIONERS HELP CHILDREN TO NAVIGATE THE TRANSITION TO SCHOOL?

The *Aistear Síolta Practice Guide* has a section on transitions, reflecting how important this area is for young children. It includes a very useful self-evaluation tool, which the ELC setting can use to reflect on how they manage transitions.

The ELC setting and primary school should share information in order to make the transition to school as easy as possible. One way to do this is to use the *Mo Scéal* templates, which are available on the NCCA website. These templates are designed to 'tell the story' of the child's learning and development and to share information between ELC settings and primary schools. The *Mo Scéal* templates are designed to capture the voices of the ELC setting, of families and of the child.

Look it up

Spend some time researching the resources and materials available on the *Mo Scéal* section of the NCCA website (www.ncca.ie).

CASE STUDY: TRANSITION FROM ELC SETTING TO PRIMARY SCHOOL

Agnieszka is the manager of Little Miracles ELC setting. It is a large setting based in a rural village, caters for children from 6 months to pre-school age and has an afterschool class.

It is the end of the year, and the Year 2 ECCE group are getting ready to go to school in September. Most of the children will be going to the school in the village and many of them will attend Little Miracles afterschool class. Agnieszka has a good relationship with the principal of the school and Junior Infants teacher. Together, they plan to make the children's transition to primary school as smooth as possible.

Questions

1. In groups, brainstorm how Agnieszka can help support the children in their transition. How can she work in partnership with families, teachers and children to ensure a successful transition for children?
2. How can Agnieszka incorporate and listen to the voice of the child in planning for the transition to school?
3. Design a poster to explain to parents how to help prepare their children for the transition to primary school.

OTHER MAJOR TRANSITIONS IN THE CHILD'S LIFE

Some children will experience major life changes while they are in the ELC setting. These changes can be happy changes, such as the birth of a new sibling, or sad changes, for example the death of a grandparent or parents going through separation. It is important to remember that no matter what the change is, it can be stressful for the child as they transition from one situation to another. The ELC setting can help support a child through these changes by:

* giving the child plenty of opportunities for open-ended and child-directed play to help them to express their feelings
* listening to the child and/or ensuring they have quiet time with their key person to give them the opportunity to talk if they so wish

- being patient if the child is acting out, for example if they have a meltdown or temper tantrum
- reading books that reflect their situation.

Partnership with parents

It is important that the ELC setting takes the lead from parents. Parents are the child's first educator. You can make suggestions, such as asking the parent if they would like to read a special book with their child as they go through the transition, but you should always be guided by the parent.

Section 3

Creating a Positive Early Learning and Care Environment

4

Creating an Enriching ELC Environment

After reading this chapter you will:
- understand the factors that create an enriching ELC environment
- understand the importance of creating an inclusive, challenging and stimulating ELC environment.

This chapter is underpinned by two documents: the Child Care Act 1991 (Early Years Services) Regulations 2016 and the *Quality and Regulatory Framework* (Tusla, 2018).

The 2016 Regulations outline the legislative requirements which all ELC settings must adhere to. The *Quality and Regulatory Framework* gives more specific detail on the core regulatory requirements for each type of ELC setting. Reference to both documents is made throughout the chapter. For ease of reading, the *Quality and Regulatory Framework* is referred to simply as 'the QRF' throughout this chapter.

Enriching Environment

It is well established that the environment is key to a quality ELC setting. The educationalists Maria Montessori and Loris Malaguzzi both described the environment as the 'third teacher' of the child, reflecting the importance of the environment to every aspect of ELC. A well-designed ELC environment is inviting to children and gives them opportunities to take risks, explore and test their emerging abilities – both independently and in partnership with their peers and adults. Standard 2 of *Síolta* states that:

> " Enriching environments both indoor and outdoor (including materials and equipment) are well maintained, safe, available, accessible, adaptable, developmentally appropriate and offer a variety of challenging and stimulating experiences (DES, 2017, p. 19). "

The standard of Environment can be understood using the following headings.

This chapter will explore the inclusive environment, challenging and stimulating environment and safe and secure premises. Chapter 5 will discuss hygiene measures for ELC settings. Chapter 6 will explore the safe environment. Finally, Chapter 7 will discuss the importance of record keeping and quality staff for the ELC environment.

INCLUSIVE ENVIRONMENT

The ELC environment should be inclusive and representative of all children attending the setting. A 'family wall' (discussed previously in Chapter 3) is a great way to create an inclusive ELC environment. The first impression a family or children will have of an ELC is the physical environment: the images on the walls and the materials and books made available to children. When children and families see themselves represented in the physical environment it makes them feel welcome and that they belong in the setting. The *Diversity, Equality and Inclusion Charter and Guidelines for Early Childhood Care and Education* (DCYA, 2016) provides guidance on how to ensure the ELC environment is inclusive and representative of all children.

> ### REFLECTION
> It is often said, 'If you can't see it, you can't be it.' Reflect on this phrase in relation to the children in your professional placement setting. Do the children see themselves represented in the physical environment and the materials in the setting? For example, are there images of ethnic minority children or children with additional needs? If not, what messages do you think this might send to these children and their families?

CHALLENGING AND STIMULATING ENVIRONMENT

A quality ELC environment is challenging, stimulating, nurturing and ever-changing as children grow and develop. Regulation 19 of the Early Years Services Regulations 2016 requires that children have adequate, inclusive and age-appropriate resources and equipment. All resources and equipment should meet safety standards.

All materials should have the CE mark, which means that they comply with European safety standards. Some materials may also carry the EN71 mark (another EU safety mark) or the Kitemark (the UK safety symbol).

OUTDOOR ENVIRONMENTS: RISKY PLAY

Outdoor environments should be designed to enable risky play. Risky play is defined as 'thrilling and exciting forms of play that involve risk of physical injury' (Sandseter, 2007, p. 248). It could involve balancing on a beam, swinging high on a swing, playing chase and running fast or sliding on a slide. Children engage in risky play naturally when they are given the time and space to do so. It is important as ELC practitioners that we facilitate this. Do not say things like 'be careful' or 'don't fall' as this distracts the children as well as leading them to doubt their abilities, become less likely to take risks and become over-reliant on adults. When children experience risk in play and try new things, they develop their independence and autonomy. To quote *Aistear*, they become 'confident and competent learners' (NCCA, 2009, p. 6). As adults, sometimes we worry that children will fall and hurt themselves. This is natural, and of course nobody wants to put children in danger. However, when children fall and get bumps and bruises, they learn a valuable life lesson: to pick themselves up, dust themselves down and start all over again. In doing this, they build resilience and become more confident in their abilities.

SAFE AND SECURE PREMISES

Regulation 29 of the Early Years Services Regulations 2016 outlines the requirements for any premises operating as an ELC setting. The premises must operate a security system to ensure that children are secure when attending the setting and that unauthorised persons do not have access. This includes:

1. **Doors/gates that lock at a height the children cannot reach:** If doors are unlocked, children may wander out of the building without adult supervision; and if door handles are at a height that children can reach, they may attempt to unlock the doors, especially older pre-schoolers who have the dexterity to undo bolts.

2. **Fob in/intercom system:** Staff may be given a fob or swipe card that they use to open the entrance door of the setting when entering and exiting. Only those with a fob can enter the building freely; all other visitors, including parents, have to press the intercom and wait to be buzzed in by a staff member. This removes the risk of any unauthorised person gaining access to the setting.

3. **Sign-in system for visitors:** All visitors to the setting must be signed in and out by a staff member.

Look it up

The Early Years Services Regulations 2016 in conjunction with the QRF (Tusla, 2018) specify the minimum physical requirements for an ELC setting, including:

* lighting
* storage
* heating
* ventilation
* minimum space
* access to toileting facilities.

Spend some time researching these requirements as outlined by both documents.

Daily checks of the outdoor environment

Outdoor environments should be checked daily for the following:

* Fences and gates are fastened shut.
* All pathways are kept clear.
* There is no sign of pests or vermin.
* Outdoor equipment is clean and free from damage.
* Sand areas are covered at the end of the day and when not in use.

Hygiene

After reading this chapter you will:

* understand the importance of hygiene in the ELC environment.

Key Term

Pathogen: the scientific term for something that causes disease. In everyday language we often refer to pathogens as 'germs'.

 Key Practical Task

This chapter covers the following key practical task:

* Hygiene: the environment, equipment and personal hygiene.

How Infection Spreads

Hygiene measures are essential to maintain a safe ELC environment that is free of infection. The Covid-19 pandemic underlined the importance of these measures, particularly as ELC settings continued to operate throughout the pandemic. Infection is caused when a pathogen (germ) enters the body and multiplies, causing illness. There are different types of pathogens: bacteria and viruses, worms, fungi, yeasts and parasites. Chapter 11 discusses some of the main viruses that pose a risk in the ELC setting. Viruses and bacteria multiply quickly in the right conditions and are spread in three different ways:

1. direct contact
2. indirect contact
3. faecal–oral transmission.

DIRECT CONTACT

Some infections are spread by direct contact with the pathogens that cause the infection. Direct contact can occur by touching the pathogen (e.g. ringworm) or through inoculation. Inoculation occurs when a break in the skin provides a direct route of entry for pathogens to enter the bloodstream. For example, a child gets a cut or a graze on their hand, allowing bacteria or viruses to enter the body.

INDIRECT CONTACT

Indirect contact occurs when the child encounters the pathogens indirectly, for example by inhalation or ingestion. Inhalation occurs when a child breathes in droplets in the air that contain the pathogen. For example, coughing and sneezing spread many colds, flus and other childhood viruses. Ingestion occurs when the pathogen is swallowed, for example by ingesting contaminated food or drink or by putting unclean toys or fingers in mouths. *Salmonella* and *E. coli* are both spread by ingestion.

FAECAL–ORAL TRANSMISSION

Faecal–oral transmission occurs when pathogens are spread from the back passage to the mouth. This occurs when a child scratches or touches their bottom and then touches their mouth, thus ingesting the pathogens. Handwashing reduces the risk of faecal–oral transmission. Threadworms, gastroenteritis and diarrhoea are all spread by this method.

CHAIN OF INFECTION

Four steps are needed for infection to be spread, as illustrated in the graphic on the opposite page.

1. PERSON COMES INTO CONTACT WITH THE PATHOGEN AND BECOMES INFECTED

A person comes into contact with the pathogen and becomes infected. It is not always obvious if a child is carrying an illness. Some infected children will be asymptomatic, meaning they do not show any symptoms. However, they can still transmit the infection. Also, most illnesses have an incubation period during which the child is infectious but is not yet showing symptoms.

2. PATHOGEN SURVIVES IN THE ENVIRONMENT

Bacteria and viruses are very hardy and can survive for some time in the environment. For example, if a child or adult sneezes on a toy or hard surface, the virus could remain on the surface for hours or even days. Even a small number of pathogens can be enough to cause illness.

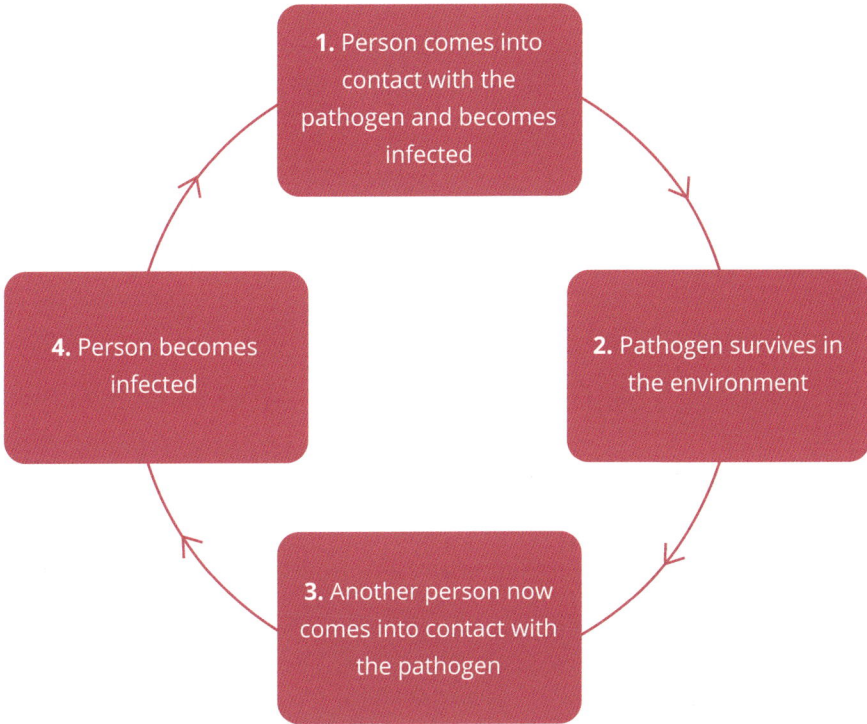

3. ANOTHER PERSON NOW COMES INTO CONTACT WITH THE PATHOGEN

This can happen through one of the transmission methods described previously (direct contact, indirect contact or faecal–oral transmission).

4. PERSON BECOMES INFECTED

This person becomes infected. Adults with a well-developed and well-functioning immune system will be able to fight off most infections without developing significant illness. However, children's immune systems are still developing, and they are at a higher risk of developing an infection if they come into contact with pathogens. This risk is increased for young children in the ELC setting.

CASE STUDY: CHAIN OF INFECTION IN AN ELC SETTING

Mary is an ELC practitioner in Little Tigers Early Years Service. Mary woke up on Monday morning with a sore throat and a cough. She didn't phone her boss to report this and instead went into work. Mary is a key person for James, Beth and Mariusz. She spent time on Monday with all three children and changed their nappies when they were soiled. Mary was coughing a lot when she was in work. She didn't cover her mouth when she coughed and didn't use sanitiser on her hands.

Questions

1. Can you identify when the steps in the chain of infection occurred in this case study?
2. What precautions could Mary have taken to prevent the spread of her sore throat and cough within the ELC setting?

Implementing Hygiene Measures in the ELC Setting

Key Practical Task

ELC settings must implement hygiene measures to prevent infection in the ELC setting.

Look it up

Source and read the infection prevention and control policy that is followed in your professional practice setting.

HANDWASHING

Childcare professionals play a key role in teaching young children good handwashing habits and to help make learning about handwashing fun. The Rufus handwashing programme has been developed with childcare professionals to teach children and emphasise the need to wash hands for at least 20 seconds and to dry them thoroughly.

Good handwashing habits helps prevent the spread of harmful bacteria such as *E.coli* which can make children under 5 seriously ill. It is important that children wash their hands often throughout the day and especially before eating; after using the toilet; after playing outside; and after touching animals.

> **Top Tip!**
>
> It can be difficult to get young children to lather their hands with soap for long enough to kill pathogens effectively. Teach children songs to sing while washing their hands to encourage them to scrub for long enough. For example:
>
> *Wash, wash, wash my hands,*
> *Make them nice and clean.*
> *Rub the bottoms, and the tops*
> *And fingers in between.*
> (Sing to the tune of 'Row, Row, Row Your Boat')
>
> *Twinkle, twinkle, little star,*
> *See how clean my two hands are.*
> *Soap and water, wash and scrub,*
> *Get those germs off, rub a dub.*
> *Twinkle, twinkle, little star,*
> *See how clean my two hands are.*
> (Sing to the tune of 'Twinkle, Twinkle, Little Star')

HANDWASHING GUIDELINES

Standards of handwashing in an ELC setting need to be higher than at home because of the large number of people in the setting. Some general guidelines include:

* Keep your nails short and clean: pathogens can get trapped underneath longer nails. Nail extensions and false nails are not suitable for everyday wear in an ELC setting. Similarly, rings will trap dirt, so they should not be worn, but a plain gold or silver band is allowable.
* Always use warm water and liquid soap when handwashing, and use a nailbrush to remove dirt from under fingernails.
* Use paper towels to dry hands and throw them away after use to prevent infection.
* Cover any cuts with a waterproof dressing to prevent infection spreading.
* Demonstrate to children how to wash their hands and supervise handwashing to ensure that they follow the correct procedure.
* Washing hands frequently may cause the skin on hands to become dry. ELC practitioners can prevent this by using a hand cream at home to keep skin in

good condition and prevent cracking or chafing, which would be a potential source of infection.

ELC practitioners should wash their hands:

- before starting a shift
- before eating, smoking, handling or preparing food or feeding a child
- before preparing meals, snacks and drinks
- after using the toilet or helping a child to use the toilet
- after changing a child's nappy
- after playing with or handling items in the room
- after dealing with bodily fluids, such as wiping runny noses, cleaning up vomit
- after handling waste
- after removing disposable gloves or aprons.

Children should be taught to wash their hands:

- after playing with pets
- after using the bathroom
- after sneezing, blowing their nose or coughing
- after touching an open cut or sore
- after playing outside
- before and after eating.

HANDWASHING PRODUCTS

Soap and antibacterial alcohol-based sanitiser gels should be used for handwashing.

- Soap should be provided in all toilets in the setting, and staff and children should be reminded to use it when handwashing. Liquid soap should be used, as bar soap can be a source of contamination. The soap provided should be suitable for sensitive skin and antibacterial soap should be provided in the food preparation area.
- Alcohol-based sanitiser gels are readily available over-the-counter in chemists and should have an alcohol content of 60 per cent to be effective. Alcohol-based gels work best on hands that are not visibly dirty; when dirt is visible, hands should be washed with soap. Children should be supervised when using alcohol gels to ensure they do not ingest the gel.

IMMUNISATION

Some diseases have such serious side effects that it is recommend that we immunise against them. For example, in Ireland, children are vaccinated against measles which was previously a leading cause of child mortality. Immunisation involves exposing the body to a treated form of the illness, which will not make the person sick but will activate the body's defence system and make the person immune to further contact from the disease. See Chapter 9 for more information on immunisation

EXCLUSION PERIODS

When a child becomes ill, they must be excluded from the setting until such time as they are no longer contagious. This is to prevent other children and staff becoming infected with the illness. Exclusion periods range from 48 hours to a week, depending on the illness.

Exclusion Periods for ELC Settings

Illness	Exclusion period
Chickenpox	5–7 days after the rash disappears
Conjunctivitis	Exclusion not always necessary
COVID-19	Two weeks from symptoms or notification of being close contact
Diarrhoea	48 hours from last episode
Gastroenteritis	48 hours since last episode of vomiting/diarrhoea
Hand, foot and mouth disease	Until the blisters disappear from the child's hands
Impetigo	Until lesions are healed or crusted or 24 hours after starting antibiotics
Influenza	7 days
Measles	5 days after the rash appears
Meningitis	Child will be too ill to attend setting
Mumps	5 days after swelling begins
Rubella	7 days after the rash appears
Scabies	Child can return once antibiotics are started
Scarlet fever	Child can return once they have taken antibiotics for 24 hours
Tuberculosis	Until no longer infectious
Vomiting	48 hours from last vomiting episode

PROTECTIVE CLOTHING

As an ELC practitioner, you will be involved in the physical care of children: wiping noses, changing nappies and assisting with toileting. When you are dealing with bodily fluids you must wear personal protective equipment (PPE). Gloves and aprons are usually used in an ELC setting when dealing with bodily fluids such as urine, mucus and vomit. Wearing protective clothing helps to prevent the spread of infection and cross infection through cuts and grazes.

Gloves and an apron should be worn for:

* changing nappies
* cleaning potties
* cleaning-up blood or bodily fluids (e.g. vomit)
* general cleaning
* handling waste.

Gloves and aprons should be disposable and thrown away after a single use.

REGULAR CLEANING

Regular cleaning is essential to maintain good hygiene in the ELC setting and will have to be completed every day. Each ELC setting will have a cleaning programme that outlines the:

* items and areas to be cleaned
* frequency of cleaning
* person responsible for doing the cleaning
* cleaning fluids and materials to be used
* equipment to be used.

Any spillages of blood or bodily fluid must be cleaned up immediately to prevent contamination. The HSE recommends the use of chlorine-based disinfectants to disinfect the area after a spillage of blood or bodily fluid.

MANAGEMENT OF CUTS

In the rough and tumble of normal play, children will get cuts and bruises. Cuts and breaks in the skin must be covered to stop pathogens entering the bloodstream through the break in the skin. Absorbent materials should be used to stop bleeding and waterproof dressings used to cover the cut. Gloves should be worn by staff members throughout.

A Safe Environment

6

> **After reading this chapter you will:**
> * understand the importance of safety in the ELC environment
> * understand the importance of an accident and incident policy
> * be aware of and practise fire safety
> * be able to assess the risks involved when planning an outing.

 Key Practical Tasks

This chapter covers the following key practical tasks:

* Dealing with an accident or an incident
* Drop-offs and collection of children
* Fire drills.

One of the questions parents ask when choosing an ELC setting is, 'Will my child be safe here?' As an ELC practitioner, it is your responsibility to make sure that the setting you work in is safe for children. As anyone who has spent any time with young children knows, they can be prone to accidents for a few reasons:

* Young children are curious about the world around them and want to explore their environment. This can lead to unsafe situations when children's curiosity gets the better of them. For example, a child interested in water may attempt to explore a pond or stream and put themselves in danger of drowning.

* Young children have no sense of danger and do not have the knowledge or experience of the world to know what is dangerous. A young child does not realise that a hot kettle will burn them, or that broken glass will cut them.

* Young children may be over-confident in their physical abilities and may push themselves too far. For example, a young child may climb too high on a climbing frame and get stuck.

The responsibility for preventing accidents rests with the adults caring for children. Adults must assess the children's environment for hazards and risks, and deal with any potential hazards to ensure children's safety. It is often said that when you are caring for children you need eyes in the back of your head, and accidents are more likely to occur when adults are distracted or stressed and not paying enough attention to the children in their care. Accidents are also more likely to happen if there are not enough adults for the number of children in the setting. For this reason, the adult:child ratio in ELC settings is highly regulated.

Adults must also be mindful of their own behaviour and safety practices. Children copy adults' behaviour – if adults are poor role models and do not model good safety practices for children, accidents are likely to happen. For example, if adults do not look right and left when crossing the road, children may copy this behaviour and risk being involved in an accident.

Finally, as already discussed in chapter 4, it is important that children are exposed to **manageable risk**. As adults, we can sometimes become overprotective and attempt to keep children away from all risk. However, this is not always appropriate. Children need to be exposed to some level of risk in order to learn good safety practices; this risk should always be age-appropriate.

Legal Requirements

Under the Safety, Health and Welfare at Work Act 2005, all employers must assess the hazards and risks in their workplace and make appropriate plans to eliminate hazards and minimise risk. This is usually done by conducting a risk assessment of the setting, which should be included in the safety statement. Additionally, ELC settings must have a policy on risk management.

Look it up

Source and read the Risk Management policy that is followed in your Professional Practice setting.

HAZARDS AND RISK

Hazard: something that could cause harm. For example, a window is a hazard if it is left open.

Risk: the chance that harm will occur. For example, what is the risk that the window *will* be left open, thus creating the hazard.

Hazards can result from wear and tear, vandalism, accidental damage, the weather and human error. It is our responsibility as ELC practitioners to limit the occurrence of hazards by checking materials in the setting every day.

DAILY CHECKS

The following daily checks should be performed.

* Plastic materials, including toys, should be checked for cracks and sharp edges.
* Metal materials should be checked for rust and chipped paint.
* Wooden materials should be checked for splinters and frayed edges.
* Fabric materials should be checked for fraying edges and to see if they are becoming threadbare.

The results of these daily checks should be documented. Any materials that become hazardous should be removed from the setting.

See page 42 for daily checks required to outdoor environments.

Accidents

Accidents are a common childhood experience. In 2018, 3,573 children aged between one and four and 918 babies were hospitalised as a result of accidental injury (DCEDIY, 2020). There are five main categories of accident that the children in your care may experience.

1. Falls and cuts
2. Burns and scalds
3. Choking, suffocation, strangulation
4. Poisoning
5. Drowning

FALLS AND CUTS

All children trip and fall from time to time. Most of these falls are minor, but some will be more serious. Accidental falls made up almost 40 per cent of the hospitalisations for accidental injury in 2009 (DCEDIY, 2020). Falls are a perfectly normal aspect of development but should be kept to a minimum.

Falls and cuts: hazards, risks and prevention

Hazard	Risk	Prevention
Unlocked windows	Child falls out of the window	Fit locks on all windows
Unguarded stairs	Child falls down the steps	Fit stair gates at the top and bottom of all stairs to prevent children gaining access
Toys loose on floor	Child/adult trips over toys	Pick up toys as necessary throughout the day
Knives	Child cuts themselves	Keep out of the reach of children
Sharp edges and corners of furniture	Child runs into sharp corners/edges	Fit plastic corner covers on any sharp edges
Icy ground in the outside area on a cold winter's day	Adult/child slips on ice	Suitable footwear. Check the outdoor area for ice before use and clear. Do not use if not safe to do so.

BURNS AND SCALDS

In 2018, 192 children were hospitalised due to contact with heat and hot substances (DCEDIY, 2020). Children's skin is thinner than adults' skin, so burns and scalds are more serious for children – and they are potentially fatal for young children. Burns and scalds are most likely to happen in the kitchen. This risk should be eliminated in the ELC setting by keeping children out of the kitchen. Hot drinks are a major hazard around children; any hot drink can scald a baby even 15 minutes after it's been made. Children should wear a high sun protection factor (SPF) sunscreen on sunny days and in summer to prevent sunburn. You should take a first aid course to learn how to treat burns and scalds.

Burns and scalds: hazards, risks and prevention

Hazard	Risk	Prevention
Kettle/saucepan on countertop	Child pulls the kettle/saucepan down on top of themselves	Keep kettles and saucepans out of reach of children
Hot drink on edge of table or countertop	Child pulls the cup down on top of themselves	Children should not be able to reach hot drinks No hot drinks in the main rooms of the setting
Hot day	Sunburn	Apply sun cream Keep children in the shade Make sure they wear a hat
Hot radiators	Child touches the radiator	Fit thermostatic valves on taps and radiators Fit radiator covers
Faulty electrical equipment	Electrical burns	Regularly check equipment for faults
Open fire in main living area	Child falls into the fire	Open fires should not be used in ELC settings Use fireguards in the home
Adult smoking cigarettes	Child picks up cigarette and is burned	Adults should not smoke around children

CHOKING, SUFFOCATION, STRANGULATION

In 2018, 657 children were hospitalised as a result of threats to breathing, including from drowning and ingestion of foreign bodies (DCEDIY, 2020). Asphyxia occurs when the airway is blocked, preventing air from leaving and entering the lungs. This can result from a foreign body being lodged in the airway (choking), because the mouth or nose is blocked (suffocation) or because the airway is blocked (strangulation). Young children are at high risk of all three.

CHOKING

Young children are learning how to regulate their eating. They may gulp their food, or they may not chew their food properly. Some foods are not suitable for small children because they are a significant choking hazard. These include peanuts, popcorn and sausages (which can slip down the throat). As you will learn in other parts of your course, young children learn through their senses. This is why you often see young children, especially babies and toddlers, putting everything into their mouths. Because of this, choking can be a significant hazard for young children. You must be careful to check that toys and materials in your setting are suitable and do not have small pieces, which a child could swallow and choke on.

SUFFOCATION

Pillows and duvets are not suitable for babies under 1, as they do not have the strength or dexterity to pull the duvet off their face if they wriggle underneath it. Plastic bags should be kept out of reach of children and should never be given to children as a plaything.

STRANGULATION

Ribbons or clothes tied too tightly around a child's neck may present a risk of strangulation. Children should never be put to sleep with ribbons around their neck, as they can get tangled. Blind cords which can form a loop present a strangulation risk for children. This has led to the publication of standards for blind cords in Ireland.

POISONING

In 2018, 390 children were hospitalised due to accidental poisoning (DCEDIY, 2020). Because children learn through their senses they are also at risk of ingesting food or liquid that is poisonous. Accidental poisoning is most likely to happen to children aged between 1 and 4. Cleaning materials or medication are the biggest poisoning risk for young children and should be packaged with a childproof lock. However, older children are capable of opening containers that have a childproof lock. Children should never have access to cleaning materials or medication in the setting. They should always be kept out of children's reach in a locked press or cabinet. At home, cleaning materials and medication should always be kept in their original container so that children (or adults) do not mistake the material for a non-toxic fluid. If a child in your care does ingest a poison, make the child spit it out, run your fingers around their mouth and flick out any remaining pieces. Contact the National Poisons Bureau helpline for advice and seek medical advice. Do not make the child vomit as this can cause further damage.

 **ABC of poisoning in children**

 Always store medicine and chemicals safely
Keep medicines and chemicals out of reach and sight of children.

 Be prepared! Know what to do …

If you think your child has been poisoned

1. Stay calm.
2. Take the poison away from your child.
3. If the poison was eaten, make the child spit it out. Check inside the mouth and flick out any remaining pieces.
4. **Never** make your child vomit.
5. If a chemical has splashed into the eyes or onto the skin, wash the eyes or skin with tap water for 15 minutes.
6. The signs and symptoms of poisoning can be delayed. Always seek medical advice!
7. Take the product container to the phone, or to the GP, or hospital.

 Call the Public Poisons Information Line

01 809 2166

Open from 8am to 10pm

Outside these hours contact your GP or hospital
or call 999 / 112

Save this number in your phone … you never know when you will need it!

www.poisons.ie   @npcireland

Poison Prevention Leaflets are available to order from www.healthpromotion.ie
ABC of Poisoning in Children 2021.© The National Poisons Information Centre, Beaumont Hospital, Dublin.
HNC00768ABC of Poisoning Poster

Look it up

The National Poisons Bureau has devised resources for ELC practitioners and parents to educate children about poisoning. These are available on the website www.poisons.ie.

DROWNING

On average 120 people drown in Ireland every year (watersafety.ie). Children, especially very young children, are at a high risk of drowning. A child can drown in five centimetres (two inches) of water because they may not have the upper-body strength to pull themselves up if they fall into water. Because of this, children should not be left unsupervised in the bath or in paddling pools. Be aware of the risks of drowning if you take children on outings to a park where there is a pond or river. Be extra cautious and vigilant of the risk that these pose.

Look it up

Water Safety Ireland has devised resources for ELC practitioners to educate children about water safety. These are available on the website: watersafety.ie/hold-hands

Top Tip!

When assessing the ELC environment, get down onto the floor and look at things from the child's level. It will help you to see things from the child's perspective for a more complete assessment of potential hazards in the environment.

CASE STUDY: SAFETY IN THE ELC SETTING

Happy Feet is a sessional service catering for 20 children between the ages of 3 and 5. Happy Feet is run by Maureen and her two staff members, James and Irina. Maureen has a QQI Level 6 Certificate in Early Childhood Care and Education. James and Irina both have a QQI Level 5 Certificate in Early Childhood Care and Education, and Irina is currently studying for the LINC (Leadership for Inclusion) Award.

There are some health and safety considerations that need to be addressed in the setting:

* The table top and block areas get very messy during the course of the day. Often toys are left strewn around the floor and the children do not tidy them up.

- Some of the toys in the table top area and block area are old – the last stock update was four years ago.
- Some of the books have seen better days – a lot of the pages are dog-eared.
- The outdoor area backs on to a local park. On Monday mornings the staff often find empty beer cans and chip papers thrown over the wall.
- The cover of the sandpit is cracked.
- There is a crab apple tree in the corner of the outdoor play area.

Questions

1. Make a list of potential hazards in the setting and how these could be prevented or overcome.
2. If you were a Tusla inspector, which areas would you be particularly concerned about?

 Key Practical Task

ACCIDENT AND INCIDENT POLICY

Under Regulation 10 of the Early Years Services Regulations 2016, every ELC setting must have a policy on how to deal with any accidents and incidents that may occur. Staff must be trained in this. The policy will include:

- a risk assessment of hazards and risks in the setting
- the steps taken to prevent accidents or incidents occurring
- the procedure for contacting parents/guardians and emergency services if necessary, if the child needs medical assistance
- details of how the accident/incident should be recorded and shared with parents/guardians.

 **Key Practical Task**

SIGNING IN AND OUT, AND RECORD OF ATTENDANCE

All ELC settings must have clear and comprehensive arrangements in place for drop-off and collection of children. This is a legal requirement under Regulation 24 of the Early Years Services Regulations 2016. The below figure illustrates some factors that should be considered by ELC settings when planning their drop-off and collection procedures.

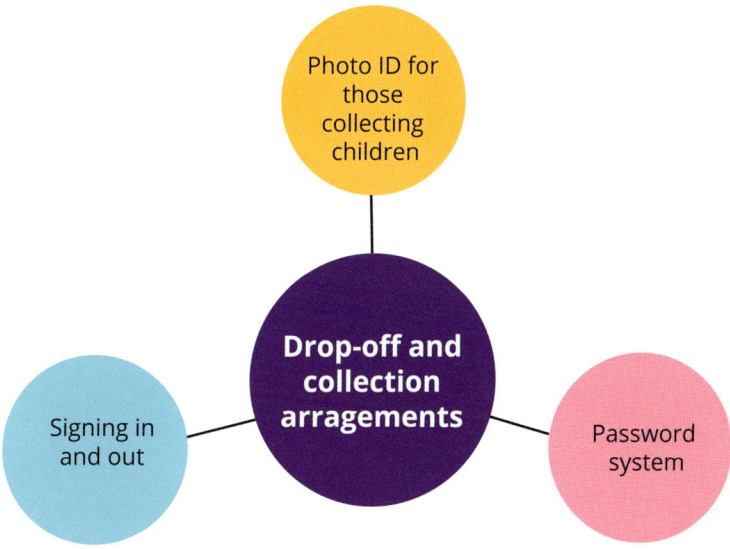

PHOTO IDENTIFICATION

When parents register their children with an ELC setting they must nominate a list of people authorised to collect the child. Many settings will require photo identification to accompany this list for identification purposes.

PASSWORD SYSTEM

Settings may also operate a password system whereby the parents/guardians of each child nominate a password that must be given to staff by the person collecting the child. Each child has a unique password, which should only be shared with people whom the parents/guardians trust to collect their child.

SIGNING IN AND OUT

A record of attendance must be maintained each day. All children who enter and leave the premises must be signed in and out in the record of attendance by an employee of the setting. All staff members must sign in and out when they come to work. Any visitors to the setting must also sign in and out. This means that if there is an emergency evacuation, an exact list of who is in the premises is available. When the Tusla Inspectorate team comes to inspect a setting, they can ask to see this record. All records must be kept for at least two years.

Morning meet and greet: Points to remember

Greet each child and their parent/guardian every morning when they sign in. Get down on the child's level and greet the child individually: ask how they are that morning and welcome them to the setting. This helps the child to feel secure and welcome in the setting. It also reassures the parent/guardian that the child will be well cared for in their absence. If the person dropping the child off is unfamiliar to you, make sure to check the password and/or photo identification. ELC practitioners can only take a child from a guardian who is aged 16 or over.

Fire Safety

Fire can spread quickly and is deadly to children and adults. Fire poses a double hazard: smoke inhalation and burns. Of the two, smoke inhalation poses a more immediate threat, as carbon monoxide poisoning can cause death within minutes.

THE FIRE TRIANGLE

Three things are needed for a fire to develop: oxygen, heat and fuel. These are represented in a triangle known as the 'fire triangle'.

Under Regulation 26 of the Early Years Services Regulations 2016, all ELC settings must have a fire safety policy. Fire can break out at any time and will cause panic, so all ELC practitioners must be trained in fire safety, and this must be renewed every two years. Every room in the setting should have a smoke alarm that is wired

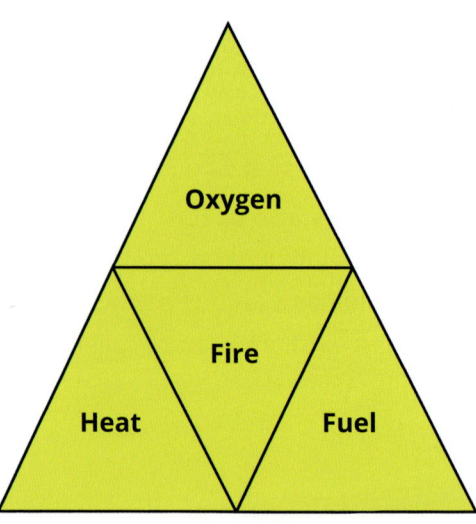

to the electricity mains. Smoke alarms should be tested at least once a month and this testing documented. Fire blankets and fire extinguishers should be available, especially in the kitchen. Fire extinguishers must be serviced once a year to ensure that they are working correctly. Candles should be banned, as these pose a fire hazard. Many fires are caused by electrical appliances overheating or by faulty electrical appliances. All electrical appliances should be unplugged when not in use and any faulty electrical appliances should be replaced. Fire doors must be kept clear at all times and must be easily identifiable and easily opened from the inside.

 **Key Practical Task**

FIRE DRILL

All ELC practitioners and the children in their care must be prepared in case of fire and have practised evacuation in a fire drill.

The ELC setting should have an evacuation procedure in case of fire, and everyone must know what to do in an emergency. The QRF (Tusla, 2018) states that fire drills should happen once every month and at the start of the school year. The fire drill should be held on different days and at different times each month. Through this regular practice ELC practitioners will be prepared to act quickly and calmly to secure and reassure the children in case of an actual fire.

* Each setting should have a designated safe area to go to in the event of an evacuation. All staff, work experience students and volunteers should be aware of the designated area. In an evacuation, staff must take the children to this area as quickly and calmly as possible.

* A designated person must be appointed to take the daily record of attendance so that a roll call can be taken in the designated area to ensure all children and adults are safe.

* When leaving the setting the group should leave in single file with one staff member at the front and one at the back. All belongings should be left behind (except the roll book and sign-in sheet). The evacuation should be conducted calmly and at walking pace.

* Before exiting the setting, a staff member should check the toilets to ensure that no child or adult has been left behind.

* The last person to leave the setting should close the door behind them. This is especially important in the case of fire – it will help contain the blaze.

- Once everyone is outside, a roll call should be taken to make sure all children and staff are safe.

- Prepare children for fire drills by using play, talking to them in circle time about what they will do during the fire drill and using teddies or dolls to role play the fire drill.

- During the fire drill, children should be reassured and praised. Remember to thank them for their help.

- After the fire drill, plan an absorbing activity to facilitate the children in settling down.

Planning an Outing

Outings are a great addition to a quality ELC urriculum. Outings help to make children aware of the world around them and promote the centre's links to the community (*Síolta*, Standard 16). Outings can also be an excellent learning opportunity for children, giving them experiences that they cannot get inside the setting and complementing the learning that takes place inside the setting. For example, on an outing to a petting farm or a zoo, children can see animals in real life, complementing the books they may have read about animals during story time in the setting.

However, taking young children on an outing requires a lot of planning and care from a health and safety perspective. Children may feel nervous and overwhelmed in a new or strange environment. Before the children and ELC practitioners leave on the outing, many hours of planning and preparation will have been done to ensure that the outing runs smoothly. A risk assessment must be completed before the outing can take place. Each ELC setting has an outings policy, and ELC practitioners should be guided by this policy in planning the outing.

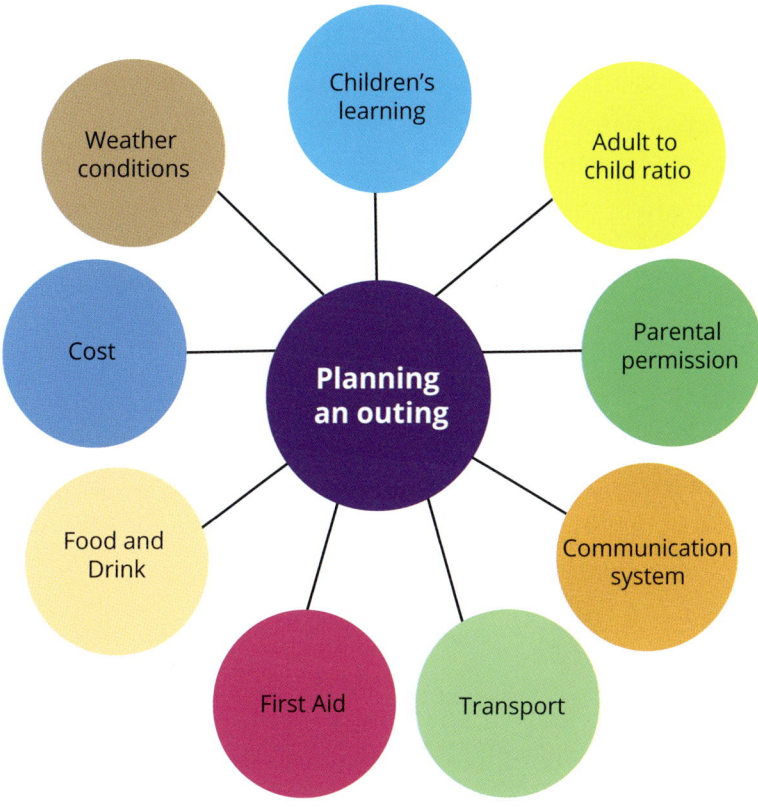

CHILDREN'S LEARNING

Outings can be a great learning experience for children. For example, on a trip to an open farm the children will learn the names of the animals and what they do, and about life on the farm. Outings should be planned using children's emerging interests and should be linked to *Aistear* learning goals.

ADULT TO CHILD RATIO

In a full-time pre-school service for children aged 3 to 6 years, the adult:child ratio is 1:8. However, if the group goes on an outing from the setting this ratio must be increased. This should be guided by the ELC setting's outings policy and a risk assessment of the specific outing. Settings can make up any shortfall by recruiting parent volunteers or students on work placement, but they must be Garda vetted before they can accompany the children.

PARENTAL PERMISSION

Signed parental permission must be received for each child before the outing. If a child does not have parental permission to go on the outing, they cannot go on the trip. The permission slip should be sent out to parents in good time before the trip, and parents should be informed where the children are going, for how long and whether there are any special requirements for the day, such as whether the children will need special clothing or a packed lunch.

COMMUNICATIONS SYSTEM

You must be contactable and able to contact parents for the duration of the outing. The setting should have a fully charged mobile phone with network access for the purpose of outings. You will need to bring a file with the contact details of parents and emergency contact details for each child in case of an emergency.

TRANSPORT

If transport is needed for the outing, it must be planned in advance. If children are travelling by bus, the bus must be fitted with seat belts for each child. If public transport is used, children must be supervised getting on, during the trip and getting off the transport.

FIRST AID

A fully stocked first aid kit must be taken on all outings and at least one first aider must be present. If any of the children are on any long-term medication, for example asthma inhalers, this must be brought on the outing in case it is needed. As always, medication can only be administered if parents have given the setting written permission to do so.

FOOD AND DRINK

According to the Food and Nutrition Guidelines for Pre-School Services (Department of Health, 2004), children in full-time day care must be given two meals and two snacks during the course of the day. If children are on an outing, these meals/snacks must be provided on the outing. Childcare providers must decide whether they will provide these or eat out. Any meals/snacks must be nutritionally balanced, with any allergies or dietary requirements catered for. Drinks must always be brought on the outing.

COST

The outing must be priced and budgeted for in advance. Settings must decide whether or not they will subsidise the outing. Remember: costs will need to be kept as low as possible for both the setting and the parents.

WEATHER CONDITIONS

In Ireland, the weather is unpredictable, so ELC practitioners should plan for every eventuality. Parents should be asked to put an all-day suncream on the children in the morning before the outing. Sun hats and suncream should be brought for each child, as well as rain jackets. Remember: there is no such thing as bad weather, only unsuitable clothing!

CASE STUDY: PLANNING AN OUTING

It is spring, and Happy Feet is planning an outing to Foley's Open Farm. Twenty children attend the service, which runs on a sessional basis. All children have been given permission to attend. Maureen, the ELC manager, is currently planning for the trip with her colleagues, James and Irina.

Maureen thinks that the outing will offer great learning opportunities to the children. Some of the children have shown an emerging interest in farms and farm animals in recent weeks, and the outing will be a great way to build on this. The outing will link to *Aistear* learning goals and *Síolta* standards.

However, her colleague James is a little worried. James knows that Foley's Open Farm is still a working farm and that farms can be dangerous places for children. He knows that Foley's is run to very high safety standards, but is also aware that he and his colleagues will have to be vigilant in case of accidents.

Irina has the job of planning the logistics of the outing. She has made a list of things she needs to consider, including adult to child ratios, first aid, planning for emergencies, and food and drink.

Questions

1. Maureen believes that the trip to Foley's Open Farm will link well to *Aistear* and *Síolta*. Do some research on both documents and identify which *Aistear* learning goals and which *Síolta* standards link to the trip to Foley's Open Farm.

2. Do some research online to identify the kind of specific hazards that James is worried about. Draft a risk assessment for the outing.

3. Make a list of the items that Irina needs to consider when planning this outing so that it is a safe and quality experience for staff and children.

Record Keeping and Staffing

7

> **After reading this chapter you will:**
> * understand the importance of sensitive record keeping in the ELC environment
> * be aware of the recruitment procedure for ELC practitioners.

Accurate and up-to-date records are essential in an ELC setting. Records help to ensure that the setting is complying with the Early Years Services Regulations 2016 and provide evidence of quality care.

Record Keeping

Regulations 15 to 17 of the Early Years Services Regulations 2016 outline the records that must be maintained and stored by the ELC setting.

* Regulation 15 outlines the records that must be kept relating to **children**.
* Regulation 16 outlines the records that must be kept relating to the **ELC setting**.
* Regulation 17 outlines the information that must be given to **parents**.

When the Tusla inspectorate team visits an ELC setting, they will ask to see these records. Many ELC settings have started to store records electronically, using tablets or other devices. This can be quick and efficient, and also reduces paper waste. All records, whether kept in hard copy or electronically, must be stored securely. Hard copy records should be kept in a locked filing cabinet. Electronic records should be password-protected. The *Quality and Regulatory Framework* states that all records relating to children should be kept for two years after the child leaves the ELC setting. Staff records must be kept for five years.

Registering children in the ELC setting

When a parent or guardian comes to register their child with the ELC setting they will need to complete a registration form. Each ELC setting will have their own registration form, but all settings are required by Regulation 15 of the Early Years Services Regulations 2016 to keep the following information on record:

* name and date of birth of the child
* name, address and telephone number of the parents/guardians, and designated contact persons who can be contacted if the parent/guardian is unavailable
* list of persons authorised to collect the child from the service
* name and telephone number of the child's GP
* record of immunisations received by the child
* an individual care plan, for example for administration of medication, which will be included with the child's records if required
* written consent from the parent/guardian to allow the ELC setting to seek appropriate medical care for the child in case of an emergency.

Confidentiality

It is important that you keep any sensitive and personal information about the children in your care confidential to the ELC setting in which you work/are completing your professional placement. This is vital to preserve the dignity and rights of the children you work with, and to maintain your own professionalism and the professionalism of the ELC setting.

ACCURATE DESCRIPTION AND OBJECTIVITY

When record keeping in an ELC setting it is important to be accurate and objective in your descriptions. This means being careful to describe things as they are. Be careful to avoid words that can be misconstrued or left open to interpretation.

INFORMED CONSENT

You must get informed consent from parents for all record keeping which takes place in the setting, including any work completed by students for college courses. Parents must consent to photographs being taken of their children and must give further consent if these are to be uploaded to social media or used in promotional material. Furthermore, the child must give consent to having their photograph taken and this must be respected. This means asking the child if they would like their photograph taken and accepting the child's right to say no.

General Data Protection Regulations (GDPR)

The General Data Protection Regulations (GDPR) came into force in 2018. This places very clear responsibilities on everyone who processes data in the course of their work, including ELC practitioners. Some general guidelines regarding GDPR and ELC settings include:

* Parents must give permission for photographs or videos to be taken of their children.
* Photographs and videos should only be taken on the designated equipment owned by the setting. Practitioners should never use their personal devices to take photographs or videos of children.
* Practitioners must always ask the children if they want to be in photographs or videos. If a child does not want their photo or video to be taken, their wishes must be respected.
* Parents must give separate permission for any photographs or videos of children to be used by the ELC setting on their social media channels, website or promotional materials.
* Remember that any documentation which is kept on a child can be viewed by them or their parent under GDPR. Thus, you must be careful to be sensitive and considerate in your record keeping. Be careful in your phrasing and abide by the golden rule: if you wouldn't be happy to have it on the front page of a newspaper, don't put it in writing.

CASE STUDY: RECORD KEEPING AS A STUDENT

Tara is in stage 1 of her ELC course. As part of her course, she has completed her key practical tasks'. Here is a sample of what she wrote in her assignment:

'Today I completed the drop-off routine for John (not his real name). I wasn't looking forward to this, as I find John to be a difficult child. He doesn't listen to what I say and always tries to get his own way with the other children. When John and his dad came in, I said, "Hi John" with a smile on my face. John just pushed past me and went to play with his friend Sophie. I thought this was quite rude and disrespectful of him. John's dad was really rude as well. I smiled and started to introduce myself, but he gave me John's bag and said, in an abrupt way, "I have to go, late for work." I think this skill would have gone better for me if I had completed it with a more friendly parent and a nicer child.'

Questions

1. Is the language that Tara used in her record keeping appropriate? Why/why not?
2. How, do you think, would John's dad feel if he read this record?
3. What advice would you give to Tara to make sure that her record keeping is sensitive in future?

Staffing the ELC Setting

The staff of an ELC setting are its most precious resource. There is no point in having a well-designed, developmentally appropriate, inclusive setting unless there are high-quality staff working there. ELC practitioners must be warm, caring and responsive to children's needs. Relationships are at the core of quality early learning and care.

The number of staff required to work in the ELC setting is regulated under Regulation 11 of the Early Years Services Regulations 2016. Staff numbers are expressed in relation to the number of children attending the setting so that there is an appropriate adult to child ratio. Students on professional placement are not counted for the purpose of the adult to child ratio.

Look it up

Research the ratios of adults to children as outlined in the Early Years Services Regulations 2016.

Focus on: Safe staff recruitment

Every ELC setting is required to have a recruitment policy. The focus should be on ensuring that suitably qualified staff are hired for the position. All staff must meet the minimum staff requirement under the 2016 regulations, i.e. they must be qualified to a minimum of QQI Level 5 standard. The service must be provided with two references for each staff member and these references must be verified. All staff must have up-to-date Garda vetting, and any staff member who lived abroad for more than six months after the age of 18 must have police clearance from the jurisdiction they lived in. All records relating to staff must be kept for five years after staff leave the setting.

Section 4

Personal Care

Physical Care Routines

8

After reading this chapter you will:

* be competent in the physical care of babies and young children
* understand how to support children and their parents during toilet training
* know how to care for children's skin, teeth and hair
* be aware of the importance of safe sleep for children.

 Key Practical Tasks

This chapter covers the following key practical tasks:

* Nappy changing
* Toileting and toilet training
* Sleep, rest and safe sleep

Key Term

Sudden Infant Death Syndrome: the sudden and unexplained death of an infant under 1 year.

Holding a baby

Before you can learn the other core care skills, you need to learn how to pick up and hold a baby. Hold the baby firmly but gently, making sure to support the head at all times. The below figures show how to pick up and hold a baby properly.

PICKING UP A NEWBORN

* Slide one hand under the baby's neck to support the head; slide the other hand under the baby's back and bottom.
* Pick the baby up gently and smoothly.
* Hold the baby against your chest. This helps them to feel safe and secure.
* Talk, chat and sing to the baby throughout to help the baby feel safe and secure.

Picking up a baby

Holding a baby against your chest makes them feel safe.

CARRYING AN OLDER BABY

By the time a baby is 4 or 5 months old, they can be carried in different ways.

* You can carry the baby on your hip – this allows them to look around and explore the world.
* You can hold the baby around the waist, facing forward so that they can look around.

BABY SLINGS

Many parents choose to use baby slings. These pieces of cloth allow the baby to be held against the parent. If using a baby sling it is important to make sure the nose and mouth are kept clear to avoid risk of suffocation.

Physical Care Routines of Babies and Young Children

Physical care routines involve attending to the physical needs of a child where the child is unable to undertake this care for themselves. Physical care routines include washing (topping and tailing) the child, supporting the child in dressing and undressing, changing nappies and assisting a child in toileting. When assisting children in physical care routines, it is important to encourage the child to develop independence and to do as much for themselves as they can.

TOPPING AND TAILING

Topping and tailing is a quick and efficient way to clean a baby. It is also very useful for very small babies who are not getting very dirty. Topping and tailing means washing a baby's face, hands and nappy area, without undressing them completely.

EQUIPMENT

* Nappy changing mat
* Disinfectant spray
* Cotton wool balls
* Bowl of lukewarm water
* Clean nappy

PROCEDURE

1. Gather the equipment.
2. Spray down the nappy changing mat with disinfectant spray.
3. Wash your hands.
4. Pick up baby and place on changing mat.
5. Wet a cotton wool ball and wipe each eye from the inner corners out. Use a clean piece for each stroke and for each eye.

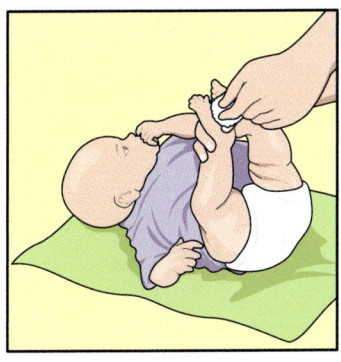 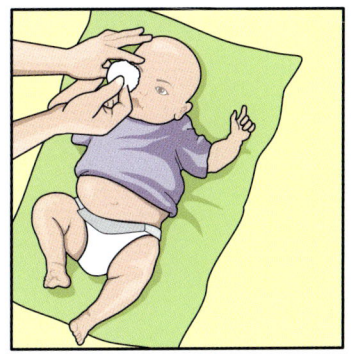 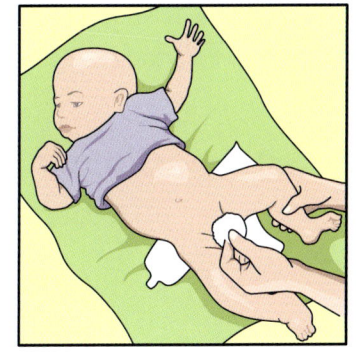

Topping and tailing

6. Using a clean cotton wool ball each time, wipe face, ears and neck, then hands and feet.
7. Remove nappy and clean baby's nappy area with moistened cotton wool balls, using a separate piece of cotton wool for each stroke. Change nappy as normal.

Safety in topping and tailing

Never use a cotton bud inside a baby's ear.

NAPPY CHANGING

Nappy changing is a basic skill that all ELC practitioners need to be fully competent in. Children will not be toilet trained until between 18 months and 3 years, depending on the child. Some children with additional needs may be late in developing control over their bladder and bowels.

There are two types of nappies: terry nappies, which are reusable, and disposable nappies. Parents will decide when their child is born which type to use for their child.

CHOICE OF NAPPY

Several factors will influence the parents' choice of nappy.

* **Cost:** Terry nappies are more expensive in the short term, but the long-term cost of disposable nappies is greater, as the terry nappies are reused.
* **Time:** Terry nappies are more time-consuming because they have to be washed after each use.
* **Hygiene:** Some parents may consider disposable nappies more hygienic, as the soiled nappies can be placed into a nappy sack and disposed of immediately.
* **Environment:** Disposable nappies are a serious environmental hazard and take 200 to 500 years to decompose. Because of this, in recent years, many parents have

chosen to use reusable nappies. It is estimated that a baby will use 5,000 nappies before they are toilet-trained.

> ### Did you know?
> 1 baby = 5,000 nappies = 1,750 kilograms of domestic waste.
>
> (Wicklow County Council, www.wicklow.ie)

Disposable nappies are the most popular choice for parents of children in ELC settings, so this chapter will focus on disposable nappies.

Disposable nappies are simple to use and to dispose of. Parents will need to supply a large number of nappies to the setting: a newborn baby can have six to eight wet nappies and one to two dirty nappies a day. There are many different brands, and parents must choose the one that best suits the baby, based on absorbency, price, and the shape and comfort of the nappy for the child. The baby's nappy must be changed every time they are soiled or wet, as well as first thing in the morning, last thing at night and after a bath. To reduce the risk of back strain, the nappy changing table should be raised to waist height.

> ### Safety!
> Never ever leave a baby unattended on a nappy changing table. They might roll off and suffer a head injury.

HOW TO CHANGE NAPPIES

 **Key Practical Task**

Standard 2 of *Síolta* (DES, 2017) requires that ELC settings have an appropriate environment for nappy changing and toileting children.

NAPPY CHANGING EQUIPMENT
* Nappy changing mat
* Disinfectant spray
* Disposable gloves and apron
* Baby wipes, or warm water and cotton wool

* Nappy disposal bag for the used nappy
* Unused disposable nappy
* Barrier cream, such as Sudocrem (if desired and in accordance with parents' wishes)
* Paper towels

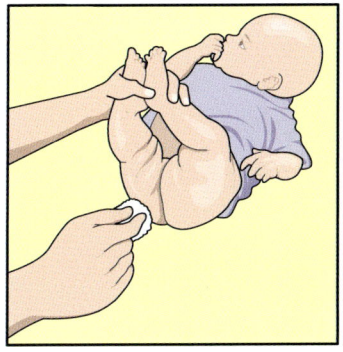
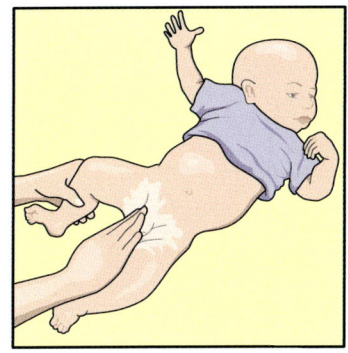
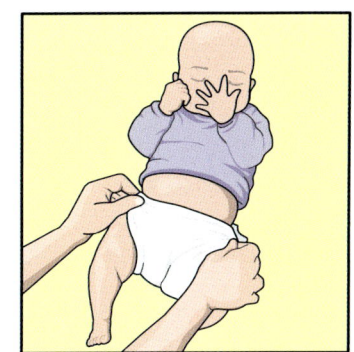

Changing a nappy

1. Gather all equipment needed.
2. Spray down the nappy changing area with disinfectant spray.
3. Wash your hands and put on gloves and apron.
4. Pick up baby, bring baby to the nappy changing area and lie them on the nappy changing mat.
5. Undo the bottom half of baby's clothes, e.g. remove trousers, unbutton Babygro and/or vest.
6. Open the nappy. Use baby wipes or cotton wool moistened with warm water to remove as much faeces as possible. Place discarded nappy in sack.
7. Use one hand to lift baby's legs, and with the other hand use a baby wipe or moistened cotton wool to remove any remaining faeces. Use a separate baby wipe/piece of cotton wool per stroke and place used pieces in the nappy sack.
8. Always wipe from front to back: this prevents infection.
9. Dry baby's nappy area (the fold of skin in the groin area and around the genitals), and apply barrier cream if desired.
10. Open out the new nappy, lift baby's legs and slide the nappy under baby.
11. Using both hands, bring the front of the nappy up between the legs. Close tabs.
12. Replace baby's clothes and remove baby from nappy changing table. Wipe down the nappy changing mat, and dispose of waste material.

> **Top Tip!**
>
> Nappy changing is a great opportunity for some one-on-one bonding time with baby. Talk, chat and sing to the baby throughout to make them feel safe and reassured.

Under Regulation 10 of the Early Years Services Regulations 2016 all ELC settings must have a policy on nappy changing and toileting children. Spend some time reading the policy that operates in your setting.

Partnership with parents

All ELC practitioners need to provide parents with accurate records of their child's nappy changing. You must note the times you changed the child's nappy and if it was wet or dry, both in the nappy changing log and the child's daily record. A copy of this record must be made available to parents at the end of the day, and another should be kept in the setting.

NAPPY RASH

Nappy rash is the name given to occasional bouts of redness, blisters and soreness in the nappy area, i.e. the fold of skin in the groin area and around the genitals. Most babies will experience nappy rash, and some can be more prone to nappy rash than others. Nappy rash is very uncomfortable for the baby, so it should be minimised by taking precautionary measures.

CAUSES OF NAPPY RASH

The root cause of nappy rash is the exposure of the bottom to urine and faeces for prolonged periods of time. The resulting dampness causes bacteria to develop, which leads to the rash developing. For this reason, children should never be left in a wet or dirty nappy.

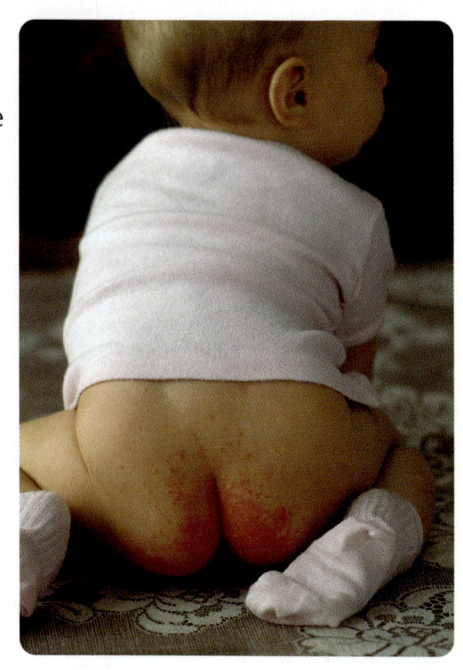

Nappy rash can also be caused by:

* a poor nappy changing technique, which does not remove all the faeces from the nappy
* friction from the nappy
* sensitive skin, e.g. if the baby's skin is sensitive to soap, bath products or detergents
* thrush, which is a common yeast infection
* other factors, such as teething or a recent course of antibiotics.

Top Tips!

The best way to prevent nappy rash is by taking appropriate hygiene measures when nappy changing.

* Babies must never be left to sit in wet or soiled nappies.
* After bathing, the nappy area should be dried carefully to prevent dampness.
* Parents should try to expose the baby's bottom to the air for a few minutes as often as possible in order to allow the skin to breathe.
* Non-allergenic products should be used that will not irritate sensitive baby skin.
* A barrier cream, such as Sudocrem, may prove useful for preventing nappy rash, but should not be overused, as it will stop air from getting to the skin.

Developing Autonomy and Independence

The psychologist Erik Erikson stated that between the ages of 2 and 3 children learn to become autonomous and independent. An important aspect of this is developing self-care skills, including toileting, dressing, blowing noses and washing hands.

ELC practitioners and other adults must be careful to encourage and support children to develop these skills. Never rush a child or tell them to 'hurry up'. Similarly, encourage the child to do as much for themselves as they can, even if it takes a little longer. When we give children the time and space to complete their physical care routines, we encourage their independence and self-esteem.

TOILET TRAINING

Key Practical Task

Toilet training is an important developmental skill for children. ELC practitioners may be involved in helping to toilet train the children in their care. As always, you must take your lead from the parents, although you can give advice and support. There is a lot of debate on the best time to toilet train children. As with so many developmental tasks, there is no right time; each child will be different. Most children will be ready to achieve toilet training between 18 months and 3 years, but in general, the earlier children start to be toilet trained the longer it takes.

Important note

You cannot force a child who is not ready to be toilet trained. The child must be ready to be trained. Parents and practitioners must take their lead from the child.

How do you know if a child is ready to be toilet trained?

* The child must be able to walk to the toilet and sit down on the toilet.
* The child should be able to describe stools and urine either using words or signs.
* The child is having regular bowel movements at relatively predictable times: this can provide the opportunity to introduce the child to sitting on the potty.
* The child is having 'dry' periods of at least three to four hours.
* The child can tell you when they need to go or when they have gone to the toilet.
* The child must have the strength and dexterity to pull their pants up and down.
* The child tugs at their nappy when wet or dirty.

- The child makes physical actions when having a bowel movement, such as facial expressions, grunting.
- The child shows interest in others' bathroom habits, and they may be fascinated by the toilet.
- The child dislikes the feeling of being in a dirty nappy.
- Most importantly, the child must not be resistant to learning to use the toilet – if they are resistant, they won't learn!

TOILET TRAINING TIPS

Just as there is no right time to be toilet trained, there is no one correct way to toilet train a child. The most important thing is to give it time and to follow the child's lead. It is recommended for parents to set aside three to four days to train their child at home. This allows the child to practise the skill in the familiarity of their home before they transfer this skill to the ELC setting.

However, the following tips may be useful.

Top Tips!

- Before toilet training commences, introduce the child to the potty during play, so they become familiar with it.
- Role play using dolls and teddies to show the child how to use the potty.
- Books and popular children's TV shows often deal with toilet training. Source these materials and explore them with the child.
- Ask the child to choose their underwear: this can be a reinforcing experience that helps to develop the child's interest in toilet training.
- Don't force the child to sit on the potty until they are comfortable. Initially, let them sit on the potty once a day, fully clothed, as routine.
- Allow the child to leave the potty at any time.
- Once the child is comfortable sitting on the potty fully clothed, let them sit there without a nappy/pants.
- Praise the child for every attempt, whether successful or not.
- Accidents will happen during toilet training – never, ever reprimand the child for these.

> ✻ During toilet training, keep the child in pants that are easily pulled up and down. Training pants/pull-up pants can be used, but some parents choose not to do so, as they think they can confuse the child. As with so much else, it depends on the child.

Developing children's independence and autonomy

Learning to use the toilet themselves is a key stage in children becoming independent. You should encourage children to be as independent as possible when using the toilet. If a child is in difficulty, you can help them, but it is best practice to encourage the child to do as much for themselves as they can.

DEALING WITH ACCIDENTS

Accidents are part and parcel of toilet training. Toddlers can become distracted or absorbed in play and may not listen to their body's signals, resulting in accidents. How the adult reacts to the accident is very important. Do not criticise the child for the accident, instead simply state in a matter-of-fact way what has happened and change the child into dry clothes. Children generally become toilet trained by day first and may take some time to stay dry at night.

Partnership with parents

The ELC setting will need to work closely with parents to support the child during their toilet training. The child's key person will need to tell the parent about any accidents that happen during the day. Ask parents if they are using any particular words for parts of the body and bodily functions, and use these with the child to ensure continuity.

TOILETING PROCEDURE IN THE ELC SETTING

Young children may need to be reminded to go to the toilet. The ELC practitioner should do this in a gentle and supportive manner. ELC settings are required to have child-sized toilets and sinks for young children. Children who are still training to use the toilet may use a potty.

Children must be reminded to wash their hands with antibacterial soap before they use the toilet. The correct handwashing technique was covered in Chapter 5. Children must dry their hands thoroughly before using the toilet.

USING A POTTY

If a child is still using a potty, follow these steps:

- ELC practitioners should wear disposable gloves and apron when toileting the child.
- Children should use the potty in the toilet area only.
- Support and encourage the child to use the potty and provide assistance if needed, while encouraging the child's independence.

When the child has used the potty, complete the following hygiene steps:

- Put the contents of the potty into a toilet.
- If any residue remains on the potty, remove this with toilet roll and flush down the toilet.
- Clean the potty using a paper towel with detergent and hot water.
- Dry the potty with a paper towel.
- Remove gloves and apron, and wash hands using antibacterial soap.
- Help the child to wash their hands.
- Put potty in a clean, dry area – do not store potties one inside the other.

Potties should never be washed in the designated handwashing sink. Potties must be stored out of reach of children when not in use.

USING THE TOILET

For children who are using the child-sized toilet, follow these steps:

- Inspect the toilet areas before they are used by children and during the day to make sure they are visibly clean.
- Children must wash their hands with antibacterial soap before using the toilet.
- Help children to use the toilet only if needed. Encourage the child to do as much for themselves as they can.
- Never rush the child or put them under pressure to 'hurry up' using the toilet.
- Children and ELC practitioners must wash their hands after toileting.

BEDWETTING

Bedwetting is defined as involuntary urination during sleep that happens more often than once a month. It affects both boys and girls but is more common in boys. Bedwetting up to the age of 6 is not unusual, as the child is still learning to control their bladder. If the child continues to wet the bed past the age of 6 years, intervention may be necessary. It is not known what leads to bedwetting, but causes may include:

* slow maturation of the nervous system that controls the bladder
* a temporary underlying illness, such as a urinary tract infection
* a small bladder, which does not hold much urine, or an overactive bladder, which gives the signal of fullness before full capacity is reached
* constipation
* drinking too much before going to bed
* a family history of bedwetting
* stressful life events, such as an illness or death in the family. Events such as this may cause a child to wet the bed despite previously being dry.

HELPING A CHILD WHO WETS THE BED

Parents may ask you for advice on how to support a child who wets the bed. You should be able to offer some tips and advice on how to deal with the situation in a positive manner.

* Protect the bed mattress with a plastic cover.
* Give the child less to drink late in the evenings.
* Make sure the child goes to the toilet before going to bed, so their bladder is empty at bedtime.
* Respond gently and patiently to accidents – don't blame, criticise or punish the child.
* Give rewards for staying dry – a star chart may be useful for showing the child's progress.
* Some parents find it useful to wake the child to go to the toilet after they have been asleep for a few hours; however, this may not work in the long term.
* The parent should also seek advice from the child's GP.

Care for Children's Skin and Hair

SKIN

Young babies do not need to be washed often, but as children grow and become more active, more frequent baths or showers become necessary. In addition, children should be taught to wash their face and hands every morning and to wash their hands after going to the toilet. Children's nails should be kept clean and short, cut straight across. Adults should ensure that skin is thoroughly dried after washing. This is particularly important for Black skin, which can easily become dry and may need a special moisturiser.

CARE FOR BLACK SKIN

Black skin tends to become dry and should be moisturised every day. Good moisturisers include coconut oil, cocoa butter and shea oil cream.

HAIR

CRADLE CAP

In the first year of life children can experience cradle cap, a thick, scaly skin that appears on the scalp. It is harmless and the cause is unknown. Washing of the hair and soft brushing of the scalp should remove the scaly skin, as will massaging oils into the scalp.

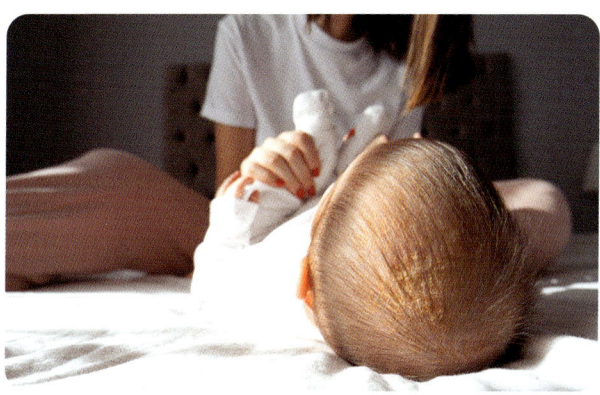

Older children's hair needs only to be washed twice a week. A conditioning shampoo may be used for children with long or curly hair to prevent tangles. Wet hair should be combed, not brushed, as brushing breaks the hair shaft.

Care for Black Hair

Black hair tends to be dry, so special hair products will be needed. Moisturising creams should be used to keep the hair conditioned and moisturised. Parents may decide to braid or put their child's hair in cornrows for easier maintenance. A scarf should be worn at night-time to reduce tangles. Black hair should never be brushed; a wide tooth comb should be used instead.

Oral Health

Oral health begins at birth: good dental care from an early age gives children the best foundation for lifelong oral health. There are three types of teeth: incisors, canines and molars. Incisors are the four centre flat teeth, which are used for biting food. Canine teeth are positioned beside the incisors and are sharp, pointed teeth, used for tearing food. Molars are the big back teeth used to grind food.

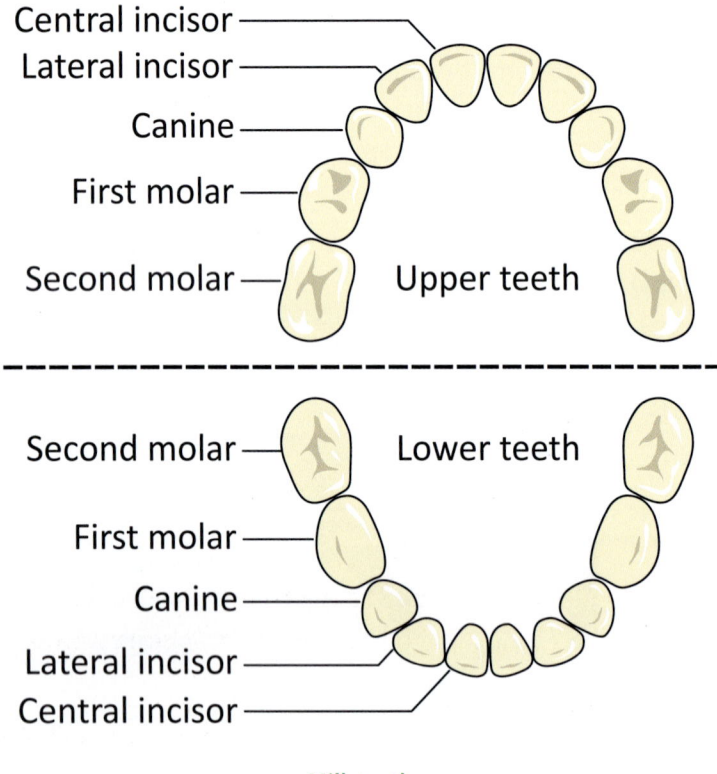

Milk teeth

TEETHING

Every child is born with a complete set of teeth under the gums. Babies can start teething from 13 weeks, although this will vary from child to child. By the time the child is 6 to 7 months, the first teeth will have appeared, and the child will have 20 teeth by the age of two or two and a half. These early teeth are called 'milk teeth' and will be replaced by 32 adult permanent teeth in middle childhood. The first two teeth to come through are on the bottom gum, followed in one or two months by the two top teeth. This pattern repeats until all 20 teeth are present.

MILK TEETH

Milk teeth are important for the following reasons:

- They help the child to bite and chew food.
- They act as a guide for the adult teeth to grow and develop.
- They enable speech and the formation of certain sounds.
- Healthy baby teeth are important for the child's self-confidence.

SIGNS A CHILD IS TEETHING

- Red flushed cheeks
- Dribbling, which may cause chafing and irritation around the neck
- Chewing the fist or toys more than usual
- Sore, tender gums around the site of the new tooth
- A refusal of food and poor night-time sleep
- Nappy rash

HOW TO HELP A TEETHING CHILD

- Give the child something to chew on, such as a cool teething ring.
- Massage gums with sugar-free teething gels or a finger.
- Parents may choose to give mild sugar-free pain relief medication at night if the child wakes and is irritable. Parents should talk to their GP or pharmacist for advice on pain relief medication.
- Cold winds can make teething worse, so the child should be wrapped up well with a hat and scarf when taken outside.
- Babies who are older than 6 months can be given carrot, apple or breadsticks to chew on.

CARING FOR TEETH

Once teeth appear, they should be cleaned with a soft washcloth twice daily. Toothpaste should not be used until the child is 2 years old, and then a pea-sized amount of child-friendly fluoride toothpaste can be used. Parents must supervise tooth brushing until the child is 7. Some children, including children with additional needs, may need additional support past this point.

Teeth should be cleaned every morning and evening. Never leave a child asleep with a bottle in their mouth, and never dip soothers into sugar, syrup or honey. Children should be weaned off the bottle when they turn 1. Avoid giving the child sugary drinks and use sugar-free medication to protect teeth from decay. The child should be brought to the dentist regularly, starting at around their first birthday.

EXERCISE

As part of the *Aistear* theme of Well-being it has been decided to hold a 'Keep your teeth clean' week in your setting to promote oral health. Working in small groups, devise a plan for the week to reflect this theme. Use a mix of activities, songs, guests invited to the setting, arts and crafts, and stories.

Rest and Sleep in the ELC Setting

Regulations and guidelines

* Under Regulation 10 of the Early Years Services Regulations 2016, ELC settings must provide facilities for rest and sleep, and must have a safe sleep policy. Look up the safe sleep policy that operates in your professional placement setting.

* Standard 9 of *Síolta* (DES, 2017) requires that ELC settings provide for children's need for rest and quiet time.

Sleep and rest are essential for health. During sleep, the cells of the body regenerate and are replenished, allowing healing to take place. Sleep is also essential for the brain to rest and to process what has happened during the day. Adults need approximately eight hours of sleep a night, but young children need much more sleep. A child in pre-school will need 12 hours' sleep, which can be made up with naps during the day in addition to sleep at night. A sleep room must be available for children to nap during the day, and rest areas should be made available for children who do not sleep during the day. Children under the age of 2 should be put to sleep in cots. Children over the age of 2 can sleep on a sleep mat, camp bed or stackable mat. Sleeping babies must always be within sight and hearing range of at least one ELC practitioner. Babies must be checked every ten minutes to ensure they are safe while sleeping.

SUDDEN INFANT DEATH SYNDROME (SIDS)

SIDS, sometimes known as cot death, is the sudden and unexplained death of an infant or young child. Despite many decades of research, it is not clear what causes SIDS. However, research has identified factors that increase the risk of SIDS. The environment also has a role to play.

Risk factors for SIDS include:

* baby being put to sleep on their front
* mother or her partner smoking during pregnancy or baby being exposed to smoke after birth – the risk increases with every cigarette the mother or her partner smokes a day and with every smoker in the home
* baby overheating, either by being overdressed or the temperature in the room being too high (above 20°C)
* sharing a bed with baby.

PREVENTING SIDS IN THE ELC SETTING

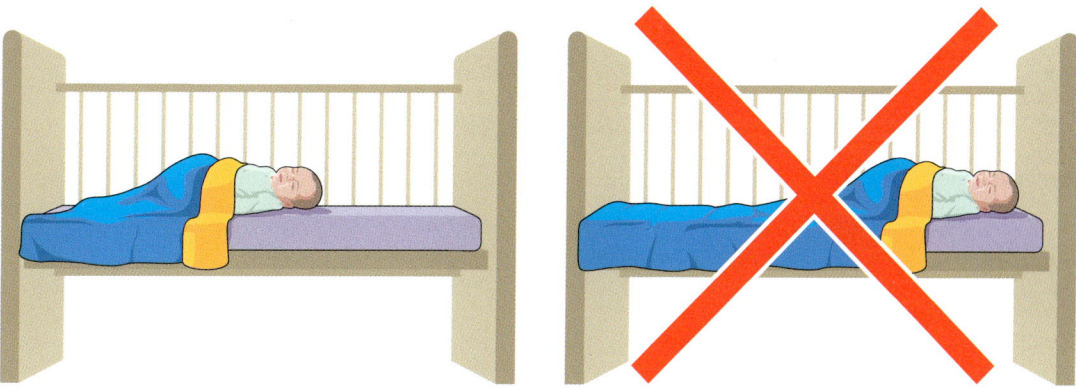

Put babies 'back to sleep' and 'feet to foot'.

A separate sleep room will be needed. The temperature must be tightly controlled and kept between 16°C and 20°C. A thermometer must be available in the room and the temperature checked and recorded every hour. Babies must always be put 'back to sleep and feet to foot'. In other words, they must be put to sleep on their backs, with their feet to the foot of the cot. This position is currently recommended as best practice in preventing SIDS. Cots should not contain pillows or duvets, as these present a suffocation hazard. Babies should be checked regularly to make sure blankets do not slip over their head. When ELC practitioners put children down to sleep, they should dress children as lightly as possible, in a nappy, vest and Babygro. Bibs and ribbons are a strangulation hazard and should not be worn by children when asleep.To help prevent SIDS, babies should have tummy time every day. This is when the baby spends time on their stomach, which is important for strengthening the muscles in the baby's stomach, shoulders and neck. You will learn more about tummy time in Chapter 13.

PREVENTING SIDS AT HOME

The same guidelines for preventing SIDS in the ELC setting apply at home. Babies should be put to sleep in a cot in their parents' room and the cot should remain in the parents' room for at least the first six months. Sharing a bed with the child is discouraged, as the baby can become overheated. In particular, the baby should never sleep in the parents' bed if:

* either parent smokes
* either parent has been drinking or has taken drugs or medication that may make them sleep more heavily
* either parent is extremely tired
* the baby is less than 3 months old
* the baby was born prematurely (before 37 weeks)
* the baby weighed less than 2.5 kg (5.5 lb) at birth.

Parents must never fall asleep with a baby in their arms on an armchair, couch or beanbag. Some research shows that giving a child a soother every time they are placed to sleep reduces the risk of SIDS, but the use of a soother will be down to the parents' personal choice.

Physical Care for ELC Practitioners

As an ELC practitioner, it is important that you maintain good standards of hygiene and physical care. This is important both in terms of supporting children with their physical care tasks and for your own professional presentation in the workplace. Some ELC settings will have specific guidance on staff presentation. Some general guidelines include as follows:

* Nails should be kept short and clean. Nail extensions should not be worn, especially for ELC practitioners who are engaging in physical care tasks with children.
* Hair should be clean and tied back from the face.
* Dangling or hoop earrings should not be worn.

* Some ELC settings will have a uniform for staff; others may just have guidelines in place. Regardless, your clothes should be clean and laundered for work every day. Dirty clothes are unhygienic and should not be worn.
* Wear personal protective equipment (PPE), such as gloves and aprons, when nappy changing.
* Make-up should be kept discreet and appropriate for the workplace.
* Shoes should have a closed toe and no heel.

LINKING PHYSICAL CARE TO *AISTEAR*

Aistear aims to help children become 'confident and competent learners' (NCCA, 2009, p. 6). Developing independence and autonomy in self-care skills is a key aspect of this. When children develop the skills needed to blow their own nose or go to the toilet by themselves, they develop a sense of confidence in their own abilities and the disposition of independence. Several learning goals in *Aistear*'s theme of Well-being relate to children's physical care including:

* Aim 1, Learning Goal 4: Be confident and self-reliant
* Aim 2, Learning Goal 1: Gain increasing control and co-ordination of body movements
* Aim 2, Learning Goal 2: Be aware of their bodies, their bodily functions and their changing abilities
* Aim 2, Learning Goal 4: Use self-help skills in caring for their own bodies.

EXERCISE

Choose one physical care task that you assist children with on your professional placement. Create a poster that shows how this physical care task is linked to the *Aistear* learning goals.

Section 5

Childhood Illness

Chapter 9

Childhood Illnesses

After reading this chapter you will:
* be able to identify the signs of illness in young children
* be familiar with the immunisation schedule for children in Ireland.

Key Terms

Signs and symptoms: A sign of illness is easily observable by the adult caring for the child, for example a runny nose. A symptom of illness is not readily observable by the adult, but will be felt by the child, for example a headache.

Immunisation: the process whereby children develop immunity to disease

Chronic condition: a long-lasting condition that cannot be cured but can be managed, and which lasts or is expected to last more than three months.

Identifying Illness

As an ELC practitioner, you must be able to identify when a child is unwell. Children will show both physical and psychological **signs and symptoms** when they are unwell.

PHYSICAL SIGNS AND SYMPTOMS THAT A CHILD IS SICK

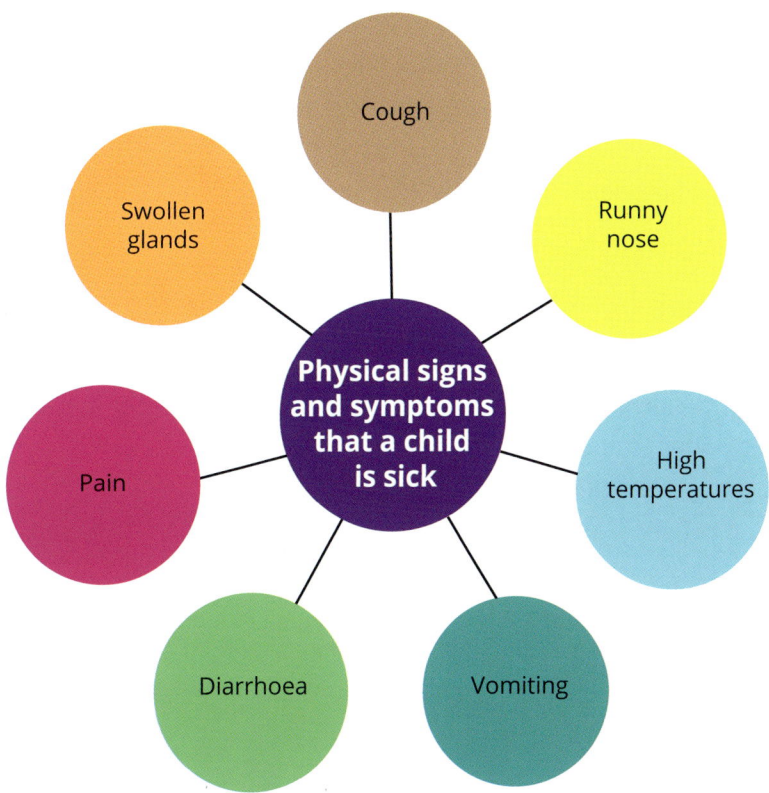

COUGH

A cough is both a symptom of disease and a protective mechanism. It is the body's natural reflex to an irritation in the throat, nose or lungs and removes any excess phlegm or mucus. Coughs can also be caused by viruses. Coughs can be classified as 'wet' or 'dry'. A wet cough is productive – it brings up phlegm and mucus that is clogging the respiratory system. A dry cough brings up no phlegm or mucus and is an irritant.

TREATING A COUGH

* At night, prop the child up on pillows.
* Honey and lemon in hot water is a good remedy to soothe a throat that is sore from coughing.
* If a cough persists or becomes 'chesty', consult the doctor.
* Children under the age of 6 should not be given over-the-counter cough medicine unless prescribed by a GP.

RUNNY NOSE

This happens when the nasal passage becomes congested with mucus, which sometimes leaks. A runny nose is usually a sign of a cold but can also be a symptom of other illnesses. The remedy for a runny nose is simply to encourage the child to blow their nose regularly to clear the nose of the mucus. Good hygiene measures should be observed, for example disposing of tissues immediately after use and handwashing in order to limit the spread of infection.

HIGH TEMPERATURE

Normal body temperature is 36°C to 37°C. If the child's temperature goes above this, it is a sign of illness and indicates that the child is fighting infection. A temperature of over 37.7°C in babies under 6 months is very serious and medical advice should always be sought. A digital thermometer will give an accurate reading of a child's body temperature. Readings can be obtained by placing a thermometer under the baby's armpit. Thermometers should not be placed in children's mouths until they are 5 or 6 years of age. Fever strips can also be used to take a child's temperature.

Digital thermometer

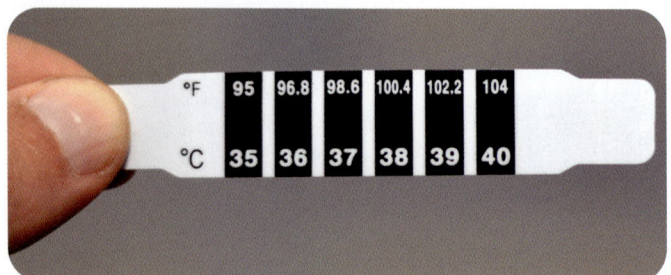
Fever strip

Children can develop a high temperature very quickly, and if a child has a raised temperature it needs to come down as soon as possible.

TREATING HIGH TEMPERATURE
The following methods can help to reduce a child's temperature:

* Sponge the child with a cold or tepid cloth.

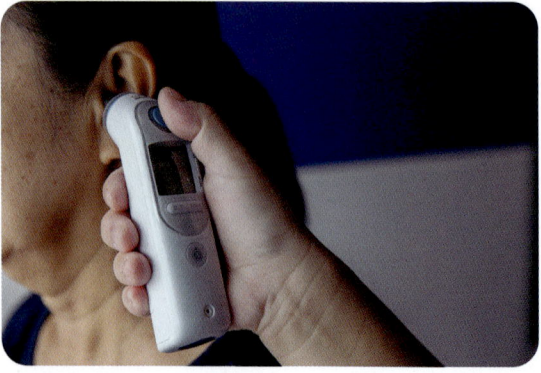
Tympanic thermometer

* Open windows to allow air to circulate in the room.

- Remove any excess or heavy clothing, bed coverings and blankets.
- Encourage the child to drink water to prevent dehydration.
- Parents may choose to give the child paracetamol to bring down the temperature.

If a child is running a high temperature and it is not brought down, the child is at risk of febrile convulsions, which are seizures that mostly affect children between 6 months and 5 years of age. They do not usually lead to epilepsy later in life. If a child in your care has a febrile convulsion, follow these steps:

1. Do not attempt to hold the child down or prevent them from having the seizure.
2. Keep the child safe and remove any items on which the child may injure themselves.
3. Remove other children from the scene.
4. Call 112 or 999 and summon the ambulance service.
5. Contact the child's parents immediately.

VOMITING

Vomiting occurs when the body violently and suddenly brings up milk, food or liquid and it is often a sign of illness. Vomiting can be caused by:

- posseting – bringing up small quantities of curdled milk after feeding
- excitement
- hepatitis
- concussion
- food poisoning, caused by the ingestion of undercooked or contaminated food or water
- gastroenteritis – often referred to as a 'tummy bug'
- whooping cough
- travel sickness
- appendicitis
- sunstroke
- respiratory infection
- meningitis
- ear infection
- stress.

CARING FOR A VOMITING CHILD

Reassure the child that they will be okay. Do not blame or criticise the child for vomiting or react in a negative manner – the child cannot help having vomited and may already feel embarrassed and upset. Get a bowl and encourage the child to vomit into this instead of on the floor. While the child is vomiting, support their head and rub their back and continue to reassure them. When the child finishes vomiting, wash their face and brush their teeth or rinse their mouth to remove the taste of vomit. Change the child's clothes and encourage them to lie down in a rest area or in bed. Keep the child hydrated by encouraging them to have sips of water. When the child begins to feel better, reintroduce foods slowly, starting with plain dry foods such as dry toast. Children should be excluded from the ELC setting for 48 hours after vomiting.

DIARRHOEA

Diarrhoea is a sign of irritation in the intestines, causing stools to be watery, loose and frequent, which may result in dehydration.

CAUSES

* Diarrhoea is a general symptom of infection and is specifically a symptom of gastroenteritis, or a 'tummy bug'.
* Too much dietary fibre in young children can lead to diarrhoea. This is known as 'toddler diarrhoea'.
* Diarrhoea can be a symptom of food poisoning.

TREATMENT

* Diarrhoea leads to dehydration, so it is important to keep the child hydrated by offering regular drinks of water.
* Hygiene is very important to limit the spread of the infection. The child and anyone dealing with the child must wash their hands. The toilet(s) used by the child must be disinfected. Any toys the child may have played with should also be disinfected in case of cross infection.
* If children under 1 are experiencing diarrhoea for more than six hours the child should be brought to the medical services, as they can easily dehydrate. Children experiencing diarrhoea should be excluded from the ELC setting for 48 hours from the onset of symptoms.

PAIN

Pain is the body's warning sign that something is wrong and is a response to an injury or distress in the affected area. Older children will be able to tell you if they are in pain, but a very young child may not have the vocabulary to do this. They will, however, show nonverbal signs that they are in pain, for example:

* pulling at and rubbing the ear
* holding the tummy
* moving awkwardly.

In babies, signs include:

* squeezing the eyes shut
* pulling the mouth taut
* squeezing the eyes together to make a bulge of flesh between eyebrows.

EARACHE

A pain in the ear is usually caused by an ear infection, but it can be a symptom of another illness, such as tonsillitis or the mumps. If pain is severe and the child has a fever, call the doctor straight away.

HEADACHE

A headache is often a symptom of illness. Headaches are often caused by being in a warm, stuffy room, but can also be caused by:

* sinusitis
* toothache
* blow to the head
* meningitis
* raised temperature
* earache
* allergies.

SWOLLEN GLANDS/LYMPH NODES

The lymph nodes produce white blood cells, which the body uses to fight infection. Lymph nodes are positioned in the neck, armpit and groin. Swollen glands are caused by a build-up of the white blood cells.

PSYCHOLOGICAL SIGNS AND SYMPTOMS THAT A CHILD IS SICK

Illness in children produces psychological effects as well as physical signs. The following are signs that something is 'not right' with a child and may, in combination with physical signs, be an indication of illness.

REGRESSIVE BEHAVIOUR

We say a child is exhibiting 'regressive behaviour' if they start to act in a way that is more suited to an earlier stage of development. For example, children in hospital may often look for a comfort blanket which they had outgrown or may look to play with toys suitable for a younger child. Regressive behaviour is often a sign that something is 'not quite right' with a child.

NO INTEREST IN TOYS

A child showing a lack of interest in a previously loved toy can be a sign of illness. Similarly, a child may have no interest in activities, toys or stories of any kind.

CHANGES IN BEHAVIOUR

Sudden changes in behaviour can be sign of illness in a child. For example, a usually placid child may become irritable and cranky, and a usually active child may become withdrawn.

IRRITABLE MOOD

When a child (or adult!) is feeling 'under the weather' they may feel cranky and be irritable. An irritable mood is often (but not always) a sign of illness.

ATTENTION SEEKING

Very young children may seek their parent's attention when sick in order to get comfort. This can show as attention-seeking behaviour, such as crying and clinginess.

Immunisation

Immunisation is a key factor in promoting children's health. Immunisation protects children against serious bacterial and viral infections. We become immune to a disease when we contract it, and our body makes white blood cells to fight against it. The white blood cells create antibodies and T-cells, which fight the infection. Vaccines contain parts of viruses, which are inactivated or weakened so they won't cause disease but will activate the body's defence system. The body creates antibodies to fight the infection and thus gains immunity against the disease. There are two types of immunity: **passive immunity** and **active immunity**.

PASSIVE IMMUNITY

Passive immunity occurs when we receive antibodies from someone else to gain immunity against illness. For example, babies who are breastfed receive antibodies from their mother in breast milk. As long as they are breastfed, the baby will be immune to whatever illness the mother is immune to.

ACTIVE IMMUNITY

Active immunity occurs when we make the white blood cells ourselves, which occurs when our bodies encounter infection. We then make antibodies to fight against the infection, which remain in our bloodstream and provide immunity against that illness.

Herd immunity occurs when enough people in the population are immunised against a disease to prevent the spread of infection.

IRELAND'S IMMUNISATION PROGRAMME

The HSE runs a free immunisation programme for infants and children/teenagers. All immunisations offered under this programme are offered free of charge. An

'Immunisation Passport', available from the National Immunisation Office, is completed for each child by their GP for parents to keep as a record of the child's immunisation history. Most childhood immunisations are given in infancy, as they immunise against pathogens that cause serious life-threatening illness. Some booster immunisations are then administered in school by the HSE Schools Immunisation team. In Ireland we immunise against the following diseases, which are very serious or life-threatening for young children:

* Polio
* Diphtheria
* *Haemophilus influenzae* type B (Hib)
* Whooping cough
* Tetanus
* Hepatitis B
* Pneumococcal disease
* Meningococcal B infection
* Rotavirus disease
* Meningococcal C infection
* Measles
* Mumps
* Rubella
* Human Papillomavirus (HPV).

Look it up

Go to www.hse.ie and research the current immunisation schedule for children in Ireland. Investigate which disease young children are immunised against. (See Appendix 1.)

POSSIBLE REACTIONS TO IMMUNISATION

MINOR REACTIONS

Minor reactions include:

- redness/soreness in the areas the immunisation was given
- slight fever
- headache.

SEVERE REACTIONS

More severe reactions include:

- dizziness
- swelling in the area the immunisation was given
- wheezing
- hoarseness.

Role of the ELC practitioner

Under Regulation 15 of the Early Years Services Regulations 2016, all ELC settings must keep a record of the immunisations that children who are attending the service have received. ELC settings cannot refuse admission to a child who is not immunised.

10

Childhood Illness in the ELC Setting

After reading this chapter you will:

* understand the legal responsibilities of the ELC practitioner in relation to medication, infection control and illness in an ELC setting
* be able to identify the signs, symptoms and treatments for a range of common childhood illnesses
* be able to define what is meant by a chronic condition and be familiar with a range of chronic conditions affecting children.

Key Practical Task

This chapter covers the following key practical task:

* Common childhood illnesses.

Link to legislation

Under the Child Care Act 1991 (Early Years Services) Regulations 2016, ELC settings are required to:

* have a policy on the safe storage and the safe administration of medication (Regulation 10 and Regulation 16)
* have a policy on infection control (Regulation 10 and Regulation 23)
* notify the Tusla Early Years Inspectorate if staff or children develop an illness from the list of notifiable illnesses maintained by the HSE under the Infectious Diseases (Amendment) Regulations 2020 (S. I. No. 53/2020) (Regulation 31).

Policies on Medication and Infection Control

POLICY AND PROCEDURE ON STORAGE AND ADMINISTRATION OF MEDICATION

ELC settings must have a policy on safe storage and administration of medication. This will:

* specify the procedure to be followed to ensure the safe storage and administration of medication to children attending the setting
* outline the responsibilities of parents/guardians and staff members in the safe storage and administration of medication.

Responsibilities of parents	Responsibilities of staff
Provide information on child's medical needs, medical history and medical contacts when enrolling the child in the setting	The child must have received the medication for at least 24 hours prior to it being given in the setting
Make every effort to meet child's medication needs before/after attending the setting	Medication can only be administered by staff members who have completed the relevant training
Complete in full the consent form for administration of medication	Store medications safely away from children's reach and according to manufacturer's instructions
Provide all the information the setting will need to: – safely store medicines – administer the necessary medication to the child – deal with any issues or incidents arising relating to the child's condition or the administration of their medication – Provide medication in original labelled container	Only administer medication that has been prescribed for that particular child
If a child needs two or more prescribed medicines, each should be in its own separate container	Keep an up-to-date list of those staff members authorised to administer medications
Parents must sign the completed medication administration form to acknowledge notification for each day that medication is required	Two staff members must be involved in the administration of medication. The dose of medicine and timing of the dose must be documented, and a series of safety steps followed

POLICY AND PROCEDURE ON INFECTION CONTROL

ELC settings must have a policy on infection control. This will:

* specify the procedure to be followed to protect ELC practitioners and children attending the setting from the transmission of infections
* include information on exclusion periods, standard precautions and hygiene measures.

> **Key Term**
>
> **Notifiable illness:** Certain illnesses are defined as notifiable illness under legislation. This means medical practitioners must notify the Medical Officer of Health or the Director of Public Health of incidents of these illnesses.

NOTIFIABLE ILLNESSES

Notifiable illnesses are either very serious and/or very rare to experience in Ireland. ELC practitioners must report a notifiable illness to the Tusla Early Years Inspectorate. A full list of notifiable illnesses is available from www.hpsc.ie. (See Appendix 2.)

An ELC setting must also notify the Tusla Early Years Inspectorate in cases of the following:

* the death of a pre-school child while attending the setting
* an incident that occurs in the setting and that results in the setting being closed for any length of time
* a serious injury to a pre-school child while attending the setting that requires immediate medical treatment by a registered medical practitioner whether in a hospital or otherwise
* an incident in respect of which a pre-school child attending the setting goes missing while attending the setting.

> **Look it up**
>
> Source and read the Administration of Medicine policy that is followed in your professional practice setting.

Common Childhood Illnesses

 ## Key Practical Task

This chapter will now outline some common childhood illnesses which you may encounter in your career working with young children. For the purposes of this section, illnesses are divided into the following categories:

* Illnesses in babies and infants
* Digestive problems
* Ear and eye infections
* Urinary tract infections (UTIs)
* Skin conditions
* Infestations.

ILLNESSES IN BABIES AND INFANTS

The following illnesses in babies will be discussed:

* Croup
* Bronchiolitis.

CROUP

Croup is a common disorder affecting children from 6 months to 3 years. It is an inflammation and narrowing of the trachea, caused by a viral infection. Croup occurs more often in the autumn and winter months.

SIGNS AND SYMPTOMS

Early symptoms include runny nose and cold-like symptoms. This develops into a barking cough and wheezing, accompanied by breathlessness. In severe cases, breathing becomes difficult, resulting in a shortage of oxygen.

TREATMENT

The GP may prescribe medication to ease the breathing difficulties. In severe cases, hospitalisation may be required.

BRONCHIOLITIS

Bronchiolitis is an inflammation of the airways in the lungs, which is caused by a viral infection.

SIGNS AND SYMPTOMS

The main signs and symptoms of bronchiolitis are:

- cough
- rapid breathing
- wheezing
- feeding difficulties.

> If a child under 1 develops these symptoms, contact the doctor immediately.

TREATMENT

A GP may prescribe inhalers to relieve the airways; in severe cases hospitalisation may be required.

DIGESTIVE PROBLEMS

The following problems are related to digestive illness in young children:

- Appendicitis
- Constipation
- Gastroenteritis.

APPENDICITIS

The appendix is a part of the small intestine. Appendicitis occurs when the appendix becomes partly or wholly blocked, resulting in infection and inflammation. When this happens, the appendix may need to be surgically removed (an appendectomy). Appendicitis is a common occurrence in young children but is rare in babies under 1 year.

CAUSE

There is no known cause of appendicitis.

SIGNS AND SYMPTOMS

The main symptom of appendicitis is an acute abdominal pain starting in the navel, moving down to the lower right side. This is accompanied by a slightly raised temperature, loss of appetite and possibly vomiting, diarrhoea or constipation.

TREATMENT

Appendicitis should be suspected if a child complains of abdominal pain for more than a few hours. Lie the child on their back and gently press the stomach on their right-hand side. If the child experiences pain from this gentle pressure and sharp pain when you remove your hand, then appendicitis should be suspected, and medical treatment should be sought immediately.

CONSTIPATION

Constipation occurs when the child has difficulty passing stools or passes stools that are hard and pebble-like. Occasional constipation is not serious; however, chronic constipation can cause problems later in life.

How often should a child pass a stool?

Every child will have their own bowel pattern, but the following table provides a **general guide** for a 24-hour period:

Age	No. of bowel motions
First few weeks	4
4 months old	2
4 years old	1

(Source: Nicholson and O'Malley, 2009)

CAUSES

For a lot of children, toileting routines can be the main problem causing constipation. If the child feels rushed or under pressure to complete their toilet routine too quickly, this can cause the child to become constipated. Constipation can also be caused by a diet not containing enough fibre and fluid. You can learn more about fibre in Chapter 13.

SIGNS AND SYMPTOMS

The main signs and symptoms of constipation are:

* hard, pebble-like stools
* pain in the lower abdomen
* blood in the nappy or staining in the underpants (this is a sign of the child straining to pass stools).

TREATMENT

* Be sensitive in dealing with the child if they have soiled their underpants.
* Do not rush the child in their toilet routine.
* Make sure the child is in the correct sitting position when on the toilet.
* Parents should consult the child's GP for advice.
* Include natural, unprocessed foods in the child's diet and reduce processed foods.
* Increase the child's fluid intake.

GASTROENTERITIS

Gastroenteritis (also known as tummy bug) is the inflammation of the stomach and intestines.

CAUSES

Gastroenteritis is a viral infection, which spreads quickly through the community. It can also be caused by food poisoning.

SIGNS AND SYMPTOMS

The main signs and symptoms of gastroenteritis are:

* vomiting
* nausea
* diarrhoea
* abdominal cramps
* loss of appetite
* raised temperature.

TREATMENT

* Stop all foods and milk.
* Keep the child hydrated by encouraging them to drink sips of water.
* Notify the parents and ask them to collect the child. The child will not be able to return to the ELC setting until 48 hours have passed since the last bout of vomiting or diarrhoea.
* Hygiene is important in limiting the spread of the infection: make sure the child washes their hands and wash down any contaminated surfaces with disinfectant.

EAR AND EYE INFECTIONS

The most common ear and eye infections in young children are ear infection, glue ear and conjunctivitis, respectively.

EAR INFECTIONS

Ear infections, which are common in young children, may occur in the outer ear (*ottis externa*) or middle ear (*ottis media*). An infection in the outer ear is usually caused by a foreign object, a boil or by scratching and damaging the outer ear. An infection in the middle ear is usually caused by a build-up of fluid in the middle ear. Ear infections are common in young children; one in five children under the age of 4 have an ear infection at least once a year.

SIGNS AND SYMPTOMS

The main signs and symptoms of ear infections are:

- pain in the ear
- raised temperature
- ears 'crackle', 'pop' or feel 'tight'
- a boil or foreign object, which may be visible in the ear
- difficulty hearing.

TREATMENT

- Medical advice must be sought.
- Paracetamol may be given upon doctor's advice to ease the pain.
- Ice-packs may help to ease inflammation.

GLUE EAR

Glue ear is a condition that causes partial deafness, and which typically occurs in young children. The hearing loss fluctuates: sometimes the child will appear to have good hearing; at other times, poor hearing. Hearing loss as a result of glue ear is temporary and should not permanently affect the child.

CAUSES

Glue ear is caused by a build-up of fluid in the middle ear. This is usually as a result of repeated infections, which block the ear so that fluid cannot drain out. This build-up of fluid causes deafness.

SIGNS AND SYMPTOMS

The main signs and symptoms of glue ear are as follows:

* partial deafness
* speech development may be affected
* poor performance in school can result, as the child may miss out on information
* behavioural changes may result from frustration of not being able to hear
* difficulty concentrating.

TREATMENT AND CARE

If it is suspected that a child may have glue ear, medical advice must be sought. A GP may prescribe antibiotics to treat the infection, but if the child has repeated cases of glue ear, they may be referred to an ear, nose and throat (ENT) specialist, who may choose to surgically insert 'grommets'. These are tiny plastic tubes that allow the mucus and fluid to drain away.

CONJUNCTIVITIS

Conjunctivitis (also known as 'pink eye') is an inflammation of the membrane covering the eyeball and inside of the eyelid, causing the eye to become red and weepy. It can affect one or both eyes and is contagious.

CAUSES

Conjunctivitis may be caused by a bacterial or viral infection, by a foreign body in the eye or by chemicals. It can also be the result of an allergic reaction.

SIGNS AND SYMPTOMS

The main signs and symptoms of conjunctivitis are as follows:

* red, weepy eye
* painful eye
* itchy eye
* eye is irritated by bright light
* eye is almost glued shut on waking in the morning.

TREATMENT

Conjunctivitis is easily treated by eye drops prescribed by the child's GP. Bathing the eye may also be useful. As conjunctivitis can be contagious, strict hygiene measures must be implemented. Children should be taught not to rub their eye. If spread within the ELC setting is evident or likely (in the Baby Room, for example), then children should be excluded from the setting until they recover or have had antibiotics for 48 hours (HSE, 2012).

URINARY TRACT INFECTIONS

A urinary tract infection (UTI) is the name given to an infection in any part of the urinary tract and may affect the kidney, bladder or urethra. Urinary tract infections are more common in girls than boys; it is estimated that 10 per cent of girls and 3.33 per cent of boys will experience a UTI before the age of 16 (National Collaborating Centre for Women's and Children's Health, 2018).

CAUSES

The main cause of UTIs is bacteria being spread from the rectum to the urethra, usually as a result of wiping from back to front after using the toilet. Constipation can also be a cause of UTIs, as can 'holding on' to urine for too long, despite a need to urinate.

SIGNS AND SYMPTOMS

The main signs and symptoms of UTIs are:

* unexplained temperature of above 38°C
* pain or burning sensation during urination
* frequent need to urinate
* strong-smelling urine
* bedwetting in older children
* cloudy urine
* lower back or abdominal pain.

TREATMENT

The child will need to see their GP, who will take a sample of urine to test for a UTI. If an infection is present, the GP will prescribe a course of antibiotics. The child should drink plenty of fluids and empty their bladder regularly. Children should be taught to wipe from front to back after using the toilet to minimise the risk of UTIs.

SKIN CONDITIONS

IMPETIGO

Impetigo presents as a red, blistering rash around the nose and mouth. The rash then crusts over to a honey colour.

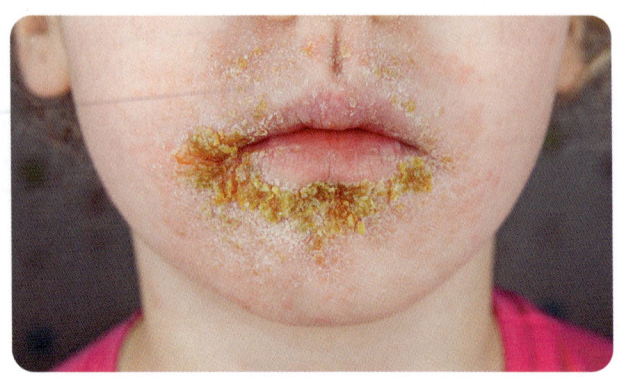

CAUSE
Impetigo is a bacterial skin infection, spread by direct contact with broken infected skin.

TREATMENT
Impetigo is treated by antibacterial soaps and cream, as well as oral antibiotics. If there is an outbreak, stop all sand, water and messy play, and wash all dressing-up clothes. The child should be excluded from the ELC setting until the lesions have crusted and healed, or until 24 hours have passed since commencing antibiotics.

RINGWORM

Ringworm presents as a rough, scaly, circular rash on the skin, groin and feet.

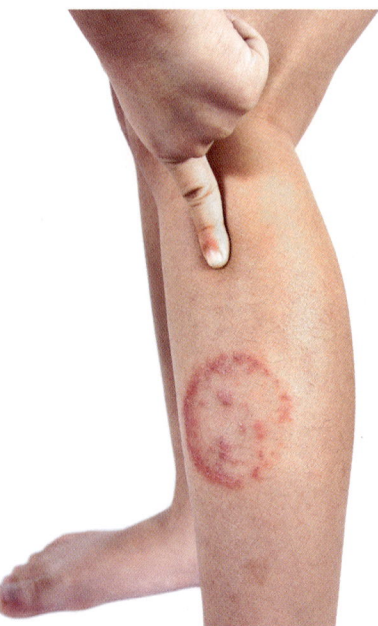

CAUSE
Ringworm is a fungal infection. It is spread by contact with infected skin flakes or by using infected combs and brushes.

TREATMENT
A combination of antifungal ointments and antifungal tablets will be used to treat ringworm. Children do not need to be excluded from the ELC setting but should be encouraged to wash their hands and use good hygiene measures to prevent the spread of infection.

ECZEMA

Eczema is the name given to a group of skin complaints that occur in response to inflammation. Four per cent of Ireland's five-year-olds have eczema (ESRI, 2019). Atopic eczema usually begins between 18 months and 2 years. The skin becomes itchy, dry, flaky, red and painful. On black skin, eczema can 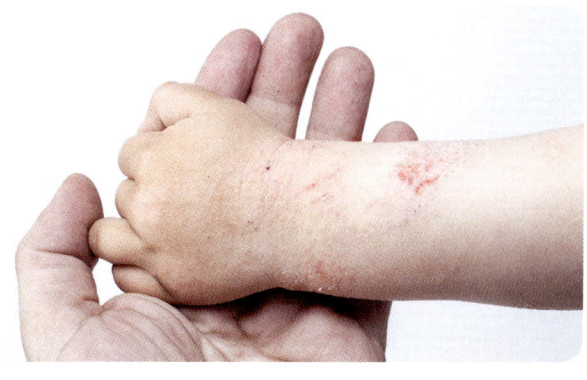 cause the skin to look a darker brown, purple or grey in colour (National Eczema Association). Eczema commonly presents on the skin creases of elbows, wrists and behind the knees. Babies may develop eczema on their face.

CAUSES

Eczema is often triggered by certain substances and conditions, including:

- extreme hot or cold
- washing powder
- house dust mites
- wool
- fur
- stress
- intolerance to dairy or eggs.

Note: Different children will have different triggers for eczema.

TREATMENT

- The child must be discouraged from scratching, as this makes the rash worse. To limit scratching, nails should be kept short.
- Dress the child in loose cotton clothes, which will not aggravate the condition.
- Ensure the room is at a suitable temperature: over-warm rooms can aggravate the condition.
- Special soaps will have to be used, such as hypoallergenic soap.
- Antihistamine cream may be prescribed by a GP and used to ease the pain of eczema.

CASE STUDY: A CHILD WITH ECZEMA

Mike is 4 and attends Little Tots Day Care full time, five days a week. When Mike was a baby, his skin was very dry and often flared up into dry, red, itchy patches. He was diagnosed with eczema when he was 2. His eczema flares up from time to time, causing patches of red, inflamed, dry, itchy skin on his arms and legs. Certain triggers seem to worsen Mike's eczema. If the house is very hot and humid, this makes his eczema worse, so the temperature of the house is controlled and kept at a suitable temperature by a thermostat. Dairy products also affect Mike's eczema, so his parents try to limit the amount he eats and try to use substitutes such as goat milk.

When Mike went to pre-school his parents met with Joe, his key person, and explained about Mike's eczema and his special diet. Joe was supportive and, with his co-workers, has arranged to follow Mike's diet in the setting. Perfumed soaps and washing powders irritate Mike's eczema, so special soaps for sensitive skin are used at home and in the setting. Mike's skin gets dry after bathing, so his parents apply emollient creams to lock in moisture. Sometimes Mike's eczema gets particularly itchy, causing him to scratch. To prevent this his parents keep his nails short, and during particularly bad flare-ups he wears gloves to bed.

In the ELC setting, messy play activities like dough, water play and gloop can exacerbate Mike's eczema. After discussion with Mike's parents, it was decided to provide Mike with gloves to wear during these activities, enabling him to join in fully with the fun. Mike's parents have given Joe permission to apply emollient cream during the day if necessary; and when Mike is on steroid cream, have given Joe permission to apply this, in line with the GP's instructions. Joe is happy to assist in this and has devised an Individual Care Plan which he marks off when the cream is administered. There are two copies of the care plan: one goes home in Mike's record-of-care book, the other is kept on site.

INFESTATIONS

* Threadworms
* Scabies
* Head lice.

THREADWORMS

Threadworms (also known as 'worms') are minute parasites which look like very fine threads of white cotton and measure up to one centimetre in length. Infestations of threadworms are very common in children, especially those aged 5 to 9 years.

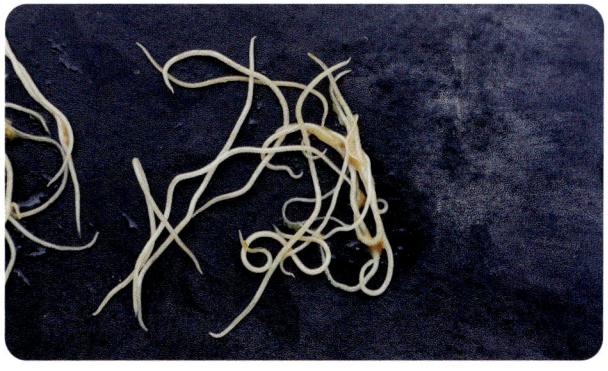

CAUSES

Threadworm eggs are usually invisible to the naked eye and are found on skin, dust, clothes and toys. Children catch threadworms by ingesting the eggs. This usually happens when the child sucks on an object or eats food that has been contaminated with the eggs. These eggs will develop into adult worms in the intestine. The worms lay their eggs on the skin surrounding the anus. The resulting itching causes children to scratch their bottom. The eggs remain under fingernails unless killed by handwashing. If the child puts their hand in their mouth after scratching, they will ingest the new eggs and the cycle begins again.

SIGNS AND SYMPTOMS

The main signs and symptoms of threadworms are:

* itching in the anal area, especially at night
* inflammation and redness in the anus, as a result of scratching
* thin, white threads may be visible in the child's faeces (these are the worms).

TREATMENT

Over-the-counter medication can be obtained from the pharmacist and should be administered to the entire family. Once the drugs have been administered, all bedclothes should be changed and the old bedclothes washed at a high temperature to kill any residual eggs. Vacuum children's play areas and bathrooms to kill any residual eggs, and disinfect the toilet area regularly. Children should be discouraged from scratching their bottom, as this perpetuates the cycle of infection. Exclusion from the ELC setting is not necessary.

SCABIES

CAUSE

Scabies is an itchy rash caused by an infestation of the mite *Sarcoptes scabiei*, which burrows under the skin to lay its eggs. This causes intense scratching. In some cases, the scratching caused by scabies can be so intense that the skin is broken.

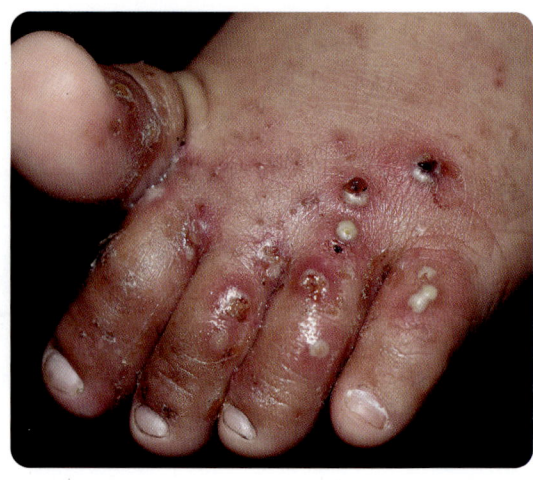

TREATMENT

A scabies infection can be treated with lotion bought over the counter in the pharmacy. The lotion will need to be applied to every member of the household and reapplied again four to seven days later. Bed linen and clothing will have to be changed and washed at a high temperature to kill any remaining mites. Children will not have to be excluded from the setting once treated, but other parents must be informed so that they can treat their child.

HEAD LICE

Head lice are small grey/brown insects, no larger than 3 mm in length, or the size of a pinhead. Head lice infestations are very common, and most children will encounter head lice at some stage. They affect girls more than boys, probably because of girls sharing combs, hats and other items. It is not known how many Irish children are affected by head lice, but it is estimated to be 8 per cent of primary school children every year (Casey and Phelan, 2008).

CAUSE

The head louse hatches out of a white shell, which remains stuck to the hair shaft after the louse hatches. These shells are what is known as 'nits'. The shell grows with the

shaft of hair and the date of infestation can be estimated by determining the distance from scalp to the shell furthest from it. A female louse lives for 25 to 30 days and can lay six to eight eggs daily, each of which will hatch after seven to eight days. Contrary to popular belief, head lice do not fly or jump from one head to another. They spread from head-to-head contact and from sharing hair accessories and hairbrushes.

Link to safeguarding

Recurrent headlice *can* be a sign of child neglect. As with all safeguarding issues, it is important to look at the full context to determine if this is reasonable grounds for concern.

SIGNS AND SYMPTOMS

* The scalp will be itchy, particularly at the nape of the neck and behind the ears.
* Nits may be visible.
* Lice shed their skin at night and leave a black dust-like deposit on pillowcases.

Head lice myths

1. Head lice do not prefer clean hair to dirty hair – they can be found on both.
2. Although head lice are more common in children, anyone can get head lice.
3. Head lice cannot jump or fly; they spread from head-to-head contact.
4. You cannot catch head lice from pets.
5. While itching is often a sign of head lice, not everyone with head lice will have an itchy scalp.
6. Head lice do not prefer long hair to short hair.

TREATMENT

* Prevention is better than cure, so parents should regularly check their children's hair for signs of lice.
* Many medicated shampoos that kill lice are available over the counter. These should only be used if lice are present in hair, as overuse reduces their effectiveness.
* Nits are difficult to remove; they stick to the hair shaft and can only be removed by combing wet hair with a fine-tooth comb.
* Washing children's hair using tea tree shampoo can prevent lice from recurring.

- Encourage children to tie back long hair.
- Any clothing or bed linen that may have been infested must be washed at a high temperature for the purposes of sterilisation.
- Brushes and combs should be soaked in hot water for ten minutes to kill any residual lice or unhatched eggs.

OUTBREAK OF HEAD LICE IN AN ELC SETTING

Many ELC settings will experience an outbreak of head lice at one stage or another. If an outbreak occurs, you must write to all parents informing them of the outbreak and outlining treatment steps. You must never name, in writing or otherwise, the children who have lice. Exclusion from the setting is not required. Discourage sharing of hairbrushes, hair accessories and hats in the setting. If there is a persistent problem, designate a special head lice treatment weekend and request all parents to treat their child for head lice that weekend.

Infections and Chronic Conditions

11

After reading this chapter you will:
* be able to identify the signs, symptoms and treatments for a range of common childhood illnesses
* be able to define what is meant by a chronic condition and be familiar with a range of chronic conditions affecting children.

This chapter will outline some common childhood illnesses which you may encounter in your career working with young children. For the purposes of this section, illnesses are divided into the following categories:
* Bacterial and viral infections
* Chronic conditions

Bacterial and Viral Infections

This section will discuss:

* Chickenpox
* Influenza
* Hand, foot and mouth disease
* Scarlet fever
* Slapped cheek
* Mumps
* Measles
* Rubella
* Meningitis and septicaemia
* Tuberculosis (TB)

CHICKENPOX

Chickenpox is a common childhood illness: 90 per cent of children will contract chickenpox before their teenage years (Nicholson and O'Malley, 2009). Chickenpox is usually not serious, but it can be serious in children with HIV or children who are taking medicine for childhood cancer. Chickenpox is more serious if contracted in adulthood.

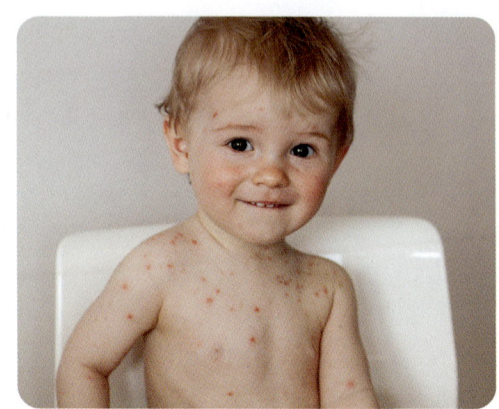

CAUSES

Chickenpox is an airborne viral infection caused by varicella zoster virus (VZV). It is spread by inhaling droplets from coughs and sneezes of those infected with the virus.

SIGNS AND SYMPTOMS

* Mild fever or headache
* A rash with small red pimples, which begins on the chest and back
* Spreading of rash to the face, scalp and arms, turning into an itchy outbreak of blisters.

Important!

* Chickenpox can be very dangerous for the unborn child. Pregnant ELC practitioners should consult their doctor if there is an outbreak in the ELC setting.
* If a child with chickenpox is hospitalised, then the Director of Public Health must be notified.

TREATMENT

If you suspect a child in your care has chickenpox, first reassure the child, then contact the parents and request them to remove the child from the setting and take the child to the doctor. The child will not be able to return to the setting until five to seven days after the rash disappears (HSE, 2012). Parents of other children will have to be notified that there has been a case of chickenpox in the setting, and this is best done by letter (see sample letter, Appendix 3). The infected child's name must not be mentioned in the letter.

Chickenpox is self-healing, but parents can make the child feel more comfortable by getting them to rest and dressing them in loose, non-itchy clothing. Children should be told not to scratch the spots, as this can infect the skin and can cause scarring. Nails should be kept short to reduce this risk. Bathing in camomile lotion may sooth the itchy rash. Temperature can be lowered by giving the child paracetamol, but never give ibuprofen to someone with chickenpox unless advised to do so by the GP, as it can cause a serious skin infection. Soothing over-the-counter creams and gels are available and can be useful to relieve itching.

INFLUENZA

Influenza ('flu') is a viral infection affecting the lungs, throat and bronchi that usually lasts one week. There are many different strains of the flu virus, so a child may be immune to one strain but not immune to another. Influenza is a severe illness, and it is especially dangerous for the very old and very young.

CAUSES
Influenza viruses travel through the air in droplets when someone with the infection coughs, sneezes or talks. Droplets can be inhaled or picked up from an object, such as a phone or door handle, and then transferred to eyes, nose or mouth.

SIGNS AND SYMPTOMS
The main signs and symptoms of influenza are:

- high fever
- aching muscles
- headache
- cough
- sore throat
- runny nose.

TREATMENT
Children who have influenza will be excluded from ELC settings for one week from when their symptoms begin. An influenza vaccine injection is available each winter for the elderly or those with an underlying illness, such as asthma.

HAND, FOOT AND MOUTH DISEASE

Hand, foot and mouth disease is a viral infection common in children under the age of 4. It causes small blisters in the mouth and on the hands and feet.

CAUSES
The illness spreads by person-to-person contact with an infected person's nasal secretions or throat discharge, saliva, fluid from blisters, respiratory droplets sprayed into the air after a cough or sneeze or stool.

SIGNS AND SYMPTOMS

The main signs and symptoms of hand, foot and mouth disease are:

- blisters inside the mouth, which may develop into painful ulcers
- blisters on the hands and feet, developing one to two days after the blisters in the mouth
- fever
- reluctance on the part of the child to eat due to the possible presence of mouth ulcers.

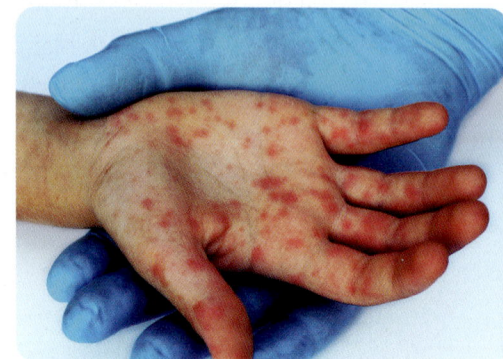

TREATMENT

The virus should last only a few days. During this time, ensure the child has plenty to drink and stays hydrated. Avoid fruit juices, as they may irritate mouth ulcers. Paracetamol is useful in controlling a high temperature. The child should be excluded from the ELC setting until the blisters disappear from their hands.

SCARLET FEVER

Scarlet fever is a bacterial infection that causes a widespread scarlet rash and sore throat. Scarlet fever was a dangerous childhood disease until the introduction of antibiotics.

CAUSES

The infection spreads from person to person via droplets expelled when an infected person coughs or sneezes.

SIGNS AND SYMPTOMS

The main signs and symptoms of scarlet fever are:

- scarlet rash on the neck, arms, chest and groin
- red spots on the tongue – these first appear on a white, furry base, but the white base will disappear within a few days, leaving the tongue bright red, which is why it is sometimes called 'strawberry tongue'
- sore throat and headache
- fever (temperature over 39°C)
- vomiting.

TREATMENT

The GP will prescribe antibiotics, which will treat the infection rapidly, with symptoms beginning to improve within 24 to 48 hours. Children can return to the setting once they have been on antibiotics for 24 hours and feel well enough to return (HSE, 2012).

SLAPPED CHEEK

Slapped cheek is a viral infection. It is characterised by a red rash on the child's cheeks, giving them a 'slapped' appearance.

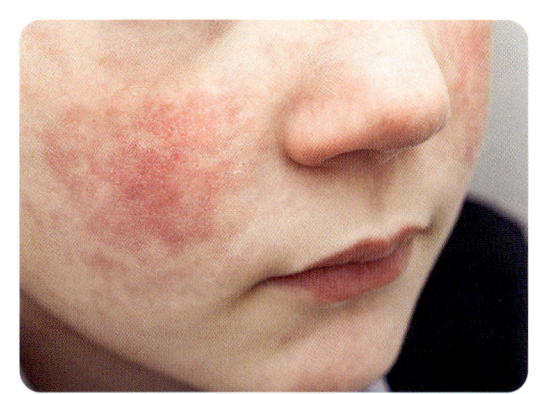

CAUSES

Slapped cheek is caused by the parvovirus B 19 virus. It is spread by inhaling droplets from coughs and sneezes of those infected with the virus.

SIGNS AND SYMPTOMS

The main signs and symptoms of slapped cheek are:

* red rash on the face giving a 'slapped cheek' appearance
* red rash on the legs and trunk
* runny nose and cough.

TREATMENT

There is no specific treatment for slapped cheek. If the child has a temperature, this should be controlled by paracetamol and the child kept out of the setting until the temperature is down. The child is only infectious **until the rash appears** and so the child does not need to be excluded from the ELC setting.

> ### Important!
> Slapped cheek can be dangerous for pregnant women and the unborn child. Pregnant ELC practitioners should consult their doctor if there is an outbreak in the ELC setting.

MUMPS

Mumps is a viral infection that causes fever and swelling of the glands around the neck. Mumps is preventable by administration of the MMR immunisation.

CAUSES

Mumps is a viral infection spread in saliva and in air droplets via coughs and sneezes.

SIGNS AND SYMPTOMS

The main signs and symptoms of mumps are:

* swelling of the glands on either side of the face, just below the ears and beneath the chin
* swollen, painful testes in boys; lower abdominal pain in girls
* pain when swallowing
* headache and fever.

TREATMENT

A hot water bottle wrapped in a towel can help to soothe the affected area, and paracetamol may help to reduce pain. Soft, liquid food should be given. Children who present with mumps should be excluded from the ELC setting until five days after the onset of swelling (HSE, 2012). Parents of other children attending the setting will have to be notified that there has been a case of mumps in the setting.

> Mumps is a notifiable illness.

POSSIBLE COMPLICATIONS

In rare cases, mumps can cause infertility in males due to swelling of the testes.

MEASLES

Measles is a highly contagious, viral infection that results in a non-itchy rash. Measles can have serious complications, such as meningitis and encephalitis, which can cause brain damage. Because of this, measles is vaccinated against (along with mumps and rubella) with the MMR immunisation. Measles is an extremely serious disease, which kills approximately one million children annually.

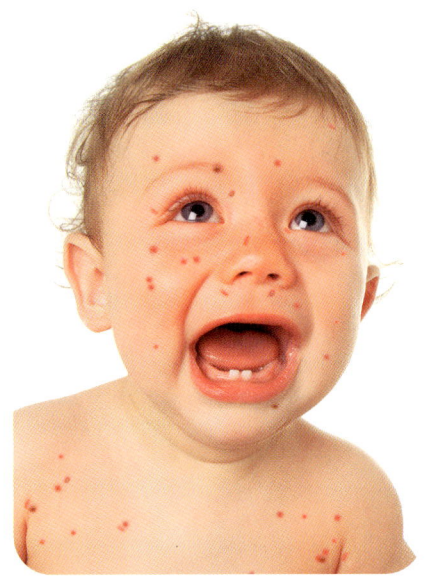

CAUSES

Measles is a viral, airborne infection.

SIGNS AND SYMPTOMS

The main signs and symptoms of measles are:

* general unwellness in the child with possibility of high temperature and fever
* flat, blotchy rash, starting behind the ears and spreading over the torso
* grey/white spots on the inside of the gum (known as Koplik spots)
* red, sore eyes
* sensitivity to light
* runny nose and a hacking cough.

TREATMENT

* Keep the child comfortable and encourage them to rest.
* If the child's eyes are affected, you may need to keep the child in a slightly darkened room.

Children with measles should be excluded from the ELC setting for at least four days after the rash appears. Parents of other children attending the setting must be informed (HSE, 2012).

> Measles is a notifiable illness.

RUBELLA

Rubella is also known as 'German measles'. It is a relatively mild illness, but it has very serious side effects if contracted by a pregnant woman. If a woman in the early stages of pregnancy contracts rubella there is a strong likelihood the child will be born blind or deaf. However, thanks to the high uptake of the MMR immunisation, rubella has been virtually eliminated.

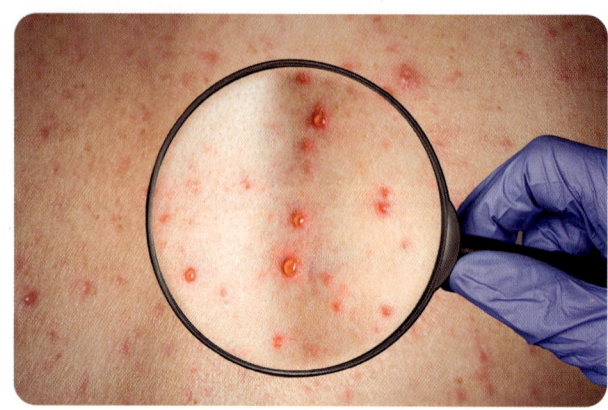

CAUSES

Rubella is an airborne viral infection spread in droplets in the air. Carriers are contagious for one day before and four days after the rash appears.

SIGNS AND SYMPTOMS

The main signs and symptoms of rubella are:

* slight fever
* swollen glands in the back of the neck and behind the ears
* non-itchy rash of tiny pink spots.

TREATMENT

There is no specific medicine for rubella and the child will recover with rest. Children with rubella should be excluded from the ELC setting for at least seven days after the rash appears. Parents of other children attending the setting must be informed (HSE, 2012).

> **Important!**
> Rubella can be very dangerous for the unborn child. Pregnant ELC practitioners should consult their doctor if there is an outbreak in the ELC setting.
>
> Rubella is a notifiable illness.

MENINGITIS

Meningitis is a serious, potentially life-threatening infection of the brain and covering of the spinal cord.

CAUSES

Meningitis can be caused by viruses or bacteria. Bacterial meningitis is usually more serious than viral meningitis. Bacterial meningitis is caused by *Haemophilus influenzae* Type B (Hib) or meningococcal type C (Men C). A vaccine is available to immunise against both the Hib and Men C.

SIGNS AND SYMPTOMS

The main signs and symptoms of meningitis in **infants** are:

* high-pitched cry
* poor feeding
* difficulty walking
* bulging of the soft spot in the head.

The main signs and symptoms of meningitis in **older children** are:

* fever
* vomiting
* stiff neck
* sensitivity to light
* severe fatigue
* signs of cold and flu
* rash that doesn't disappear under pressure (the glass test)
* temperature.

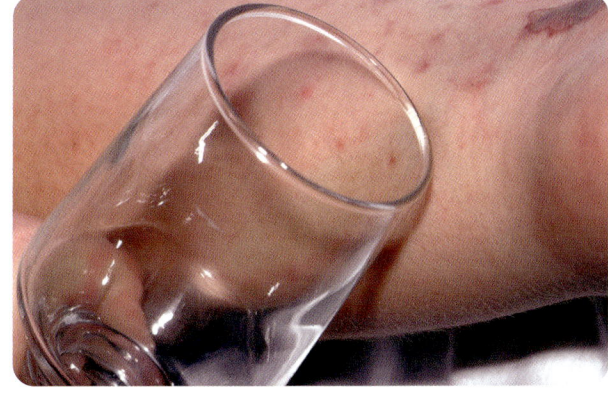

The rash that is associated with meningitis is actually a sign of **septicaemia**, or blood poisoning. This occurs when bacteria release toxins into the blood, damaging the blood vessel walls, which allows blood to leak out, causing the rash. The main sign of septicaemia is a rash that does not disappear under pressure (the glass test).

TREATMENT

Meningitis is a potentially fatal condition. If a child in your care exhibits any of the signs of meningitis, emergency medical care should be sought at once. Parents of other children attending the setting will have to be informed of the case.

> Meningitis is a notifiable illness.

TUBERCULOSIS

Tuberculosis (TB) is a bacterial infection affecting the lungs. In the past, TB was a major cause of death and disability in Ireland, but immunisation has all but eliminated TB here.

CAUSES

It is spread from person to person through microscopic droplets released into the air. This can happen when someone with the untreated, active form of tuberculosis coughs, speaks, sneezes, spits, laughs or sings.

SIGNS AND SYMPTOMS

The main signs and symptoms of TB are:

* a cough – this is the first sign, and it becomes persistent
* chest pain when inhaling deeply
* shortness of breath
* fever
* poor appetite and weight loss
* sweating at night
* tiredness
* coughing up green or yellow mucus, which may be streaked in blood.

A chest x-ray or a computerised tomography (CT) scan for lung damage can diagnose TB.

TREATMENT

Treatment for TB is through the administration of anti-tuberculosis drugs for at least six months. This treatment can usually take place at home, unless the child is very ill. The child will have to be excluded from the setting until they are no longer infectious. All those in contact with the child will have to be screened for TB.

TB is a notifiable illness.

Chronic Conditions

A chronic condition is a long-lasting condition that cannot be cured but can be managed, and which lasts or is expected to last more than three months. Examples of chronic conditions include cystic fibrosis, asthma, diabetes, eczema and any long-term medical condition. A chronic condition can potentially affect a child physically, intellectually, socially and emotionally.

PHYSICAL EFFECTS

The child may experience delayed growth and developmental delay, especially if they are hospitalised for long periods of time. In the case of some chronic conditions, such as cystic fibrosis, the child may be at risk of a nutritional deficiency. A nutritionist may be assigned to help balance the child's diet.

INTELLECTUAL EFFECTS

If the child is in and out of hospital frequently, they may miss schooling, leading to delayed development of literacy and numeracy skills. Disrupted education may also lead to the child falling behind in school. Children's hospitals such as Temple Street do provide teachers and education for patients, however, attendance is dependent on the child's health.

SOCIAL AND EMOTIONAL EFFECTS

Because of frequent absences from school, the child may have lower confidence in making and sustaining friendships. Parents may be overprotective of children, and this may lead to delayed development of independent living skills. Emotional development may be delayed, leading to regressive behaviour, behaviour problems and poor self-esteem.

If you are caring for a child with chronic condition in an ELC setting, the following steps should be taken:

* Ensure the key person system is in place: a key person is vital to help the child to feel secure in the setting.
* Allow the child to express their feelings, and provide activities that can help the child to release tensions and frustration.
* Always find time to listen to the child.
* Support the family.

ASTHMA

Asthma is a chronic condition that affects breathing. It causes the airways of the lungs to become oversensitive to triggers such as dust, which makes the airways go into spasm, causing breathing difficulties. This spasm is known as an asthma attack. Ireland has the fourth-highest rate of asthma in the world (Asthma Society of Ireland website, www.asthma.ie). According to the 'Growing Up in Ireland' study (www.growingup.ie, 2019), 8 per cent of five-year-olds in Ireland have asthma. It is not known exactly what causes asthma, but possible causes are thought to include:

* increased pollution in the environment
* low birth weight
* smoking in pregnancy
* children spending more time inside.

There are certain substances that act as triggers and can bring on an asthma attack. Different children will have different triggers, but known triggers include:

* dust mites
* pollen
* certain food
* coughs/colds
* exercise
* stress
* humidity
* mould
* changes in the weather.

Children with asthma will carry inhalers to be used in the event of an asthma attack. There are two types of inhaler: preventers and relievers. Preventer inhalers are brown and are taken to prevent asthma attacks. Reliever inhalers are blue and are to be administered to the child if they have an asthma attack. The reliever inhaler will ease the airways and make breathing

easier. If you are caring for a child with asthma, you will have to know how to deal with an asthma attack. Parents will provide guidance, but here are some general pointers:

* Reassure the child.
* Give the child their inhaler – young children may use a spacer.
* Send for help.
* Sit the child upright and leaning forward.
* Document the attack and inform parents.

Although some children grow out of asthma, it is a chronic condition that cannot be cured. However, steps can be taken to control asthma and lessen the likelihood of an attack. The following are some guidelines for controlling asthma:

* Vacuum the child's mattress, pillow and the base of their bed.
* Quilts and duvets should contain synthetic filling, not feathers.
* Damp dust the skirting boards, windowsills and floors every week.
* Wash bedroom soft fittings every week.

CASE STUDY: CHILD WITH ASTHMA

Alice had repeated chest infections as a baby, resulting in hospitalisation on two occasions. She had frequent episodes of wheezing and coughing. Alice's GP prescribed inhalers, but a definitive diagnosis of asthma was not made until Alice was 6. Alice now uses a preventer and a reliever inhaler. Her mother administers the preventer inhaler every morning to help keep the airways clear. Alice carries the reliever inhaler on her in case she starts to have an asthma attack when she is out and about.

When Alice was younger, her mother administered her inhalers using a spacer, but now Alice is beginning to take responsibility for her condition. She has learned to identify the signs that she needs a 'puff': tightening of the chest and shortness of breath. She then takes the inhaler, under adult supervision. Some things make Alice's asthma worse. She can feel worse when the seasons change in spring and autumn, and in summer if the pollen count is high. Dust mites worsen Alice's asthma, so her parents make sure to keep the house dust free, vacuuming at least three times a week and washing her bedding once a week. They got rid of any heavy carpets in the house and keep soft toys to a minimum. Alice has recently joined the under 8 football team. Her parents make sure to give her the preventer inhaler before training and to stay for the session in case she needs her reliever inhaler.

DIABETES

Diabetes occurs when the body is unable to regulate the amount of sugar in the bloodstream. This may be because the body is not producing enough insulin (a chemical that regulates blood sugar level), or because the body is not processing insulin effectively.

CAUSES

There are two types of diabetes: **type 1** diabetes is caused by genetic factors and occurs when the pancreas does not produce insulin; **type 2** diabetes can be caused by being overweight.

TREATMENT

Diabetes is treated by a combination of diet and medication. Children who are diabetic will have to follow a reduced sugar diet (explained in more detail in chapter 13). Some children will also need to take insulin before eating. Insulin is injected, and as children get older, they will be able to administer this themselves, but if you are caring for a young child with diabetes you will have to administer the insulin for them. Parents will advise and provide training on how to do this.

HYPOGLYCAEMIA

Hypoglycaemia (also known as a 'hypo') is caused by low blood sugar, usually resulting from skipping meals or not eating enough. If the child has a hypoglycaemic attack they will feel:

* shaky and weak
* lightheaded
* sleepy and dizzy
* nervous and anxious
* grouchy
* confused.

If the child is hypoglycaemic, they need sugar quickly to stabilise their blood sugar levels. Give the child **one** of the following:

* a third to half of a glass of a sugary drink, such as Lucozade or 7up
* 200 ml of fruit juice
* 2 teaspoons of sugar.

GlucoGel can be given to a child who is experiencing a mild to moderate hypo who refuses to drink, or who has nausea or is vomiting.

If symptoms do not improve within 10 to 15 minutes, repeat the treatment. Parents should always be informed if their child has had a hypo. The child may need to eat more post-hypo.

Note: If the child engages in unexpected physical activity, they will need to take in extra food to prevent a hypo.

HYPERGLYCAEMIA

Hyperglycaemia is caused by too much sugar in the bloodstream, usually as a result of missing an insulin injection. Hyperglycaemia is potentially life-threatening. Symptoms include the following:

* looking flushed
* feeling unwell
* feeling grumpy
* going to the toilet a lot
* no energy.

Important!

If the child appears to be experiencing high blood sugar levels, notify the parents. They may need to consult their GP about their child's insulin dose. If the child seems sleepy or lethargic, contact the ambulance or call for medical assistance as per the child's individual care plan.

EXERCISE

You are working as an ELC practitioner in the Toddler Room of a busy ELC setting. Sam, aged 2, has been pale all day and seems 'off form'. Sam's dad mentioned at drop-off that Sam had a poor night's sleep last night. During the morning, Sam was irritable and clinging to you. He did not eat his lunch. Just after lunchtime, Sam vomited and started to cry.

Questions

1. Make a list of the actions you will need to take to reassure, comfort and care for Sam.
2. What hygiene measures will you need to implement in the room?

Section 6

Nutrition

Nutrition for Babies

12

After reading this chapter you will:
* understand the advantages and disadvantages of breastfeeding and bottle-feeding
* be able to practise the skills of bottle making and sterilising
* be able to demonstrate the skill of bottle-feeding
* be able to outline the steps involved in weaning a baby on to solids.

 Key Practical Tasks

This chapter covers the following key practical tasks:
* Bottle-feeding and sterilising
* Mealtimes for babies.

Key Terms

Colostrum: the first breastmilk produced by the mother. Colostrum is high in antibodies.

Sterilising: the process to remove harmful bacteria that a baby's developing immune system cannot yet deal with

Weaning: the term given to the gradual introduction of solid foods into the baby's diet.

All children need the right nutrition to grow healthy and strong. This chapter will teach you about nutrition for babies. Babies grow at a rapid rate, so it is really important that parents and ELC practitioners spend time planning how to meet their nutritional needs.

Breastfeeding and Bottle-feeding

One of the first decisions new parents must make is whether to breastfeed or bottle-feed their newborn baby. When formula milk was first introduced, breastfeeding went somewhat out of fashion, and between 1981 and 1991 the rate of breastfeeding in Ireland was 32 per cent (Department of Health and Children – DoHC, 2005). However, over the last 20 years, public health campaigns have encouraged a higher rate of breastfeeding. Now, up to 60 per cent of Irish mothers breastfeed (HSE, 2019). Mothers who have studied to third level are most likely to breastfeed their children. However, Irish mothers still do not breastfeed as much as mothers in the rest of Europe, and half of those who do breastfeed stop within the first three months, far earlier than the World Health Organization's (WHO) recommended period of two years. Many children will be using formula feed by the time they enrol in an ELC setting, so this chapter will teach you how to make up a bottle of formula feed as well as how to promote breastfeeding.

Did you know?

The Maternity Protection (Amendment) Act 2004 entitles breastfeeding mothers either to breastfeeding breaks in the workplace, where suitable facilities are provided, or to a reduction of one working hour per day, without loss of pay, for up to 26 weeks after birth.

EXERCISE

Make a poster to promote breastfeeding to new or expectant mothers.

BREASTFEEDING

Breast milk is the baby's natural and preferred food choice. Human milk is tailor-made for babies' nutritional needs and contains just the right amount of protein, carbohydrates, minerals and vitamins to sustain the growing baby. It is thus recommended that all new mothers breastfeed, even if only for a short period of time. The first milk the mother produces is called colostrum, a yellow liquid high in beta carotene, protein and antibodies. Colostrum helps to kick-start the baby's immune system.

STORAGE OF BREAST MILK

Many mothers choose to express breast milk into a bottle by using a breast pump. This is useful, as it means that an adult other than the mother can feed the child and that breastfeeding can continue when the mother returns to work. Expressed breast milk can be stored at room temperature for up to six hours or in a fridge for up to five days. It can also be frozen and stored for up to three months. If breast milk has been frozen it should be thawed slowly in the fridge. A microwave should never be used to thaw frozen breast milk as this can lead to 'hot spots' forming in the milk.

ADVANTAGES OF BREASTFEEDING

* Breast milk is convenient, economical and time-efficient with regard to preparation; there is no need to make up formula milk or to sterilise feeding equipment (unless the mother is expressing milk into bottles). This makes breastfeeding a far more efficient feeding choice.
* It is produced at body temperature, so it is always the right temperature for feeding.
* It is digested more quickly and easily than cow's milk or formula milk.
* Babies who are breastfed pass fewer stools, are less likely to get constipated and are less prone to nappy rash.

LONG-TERM HEALTH BENEFITS OF BREASTFEEDING

Recent research investigating the potential long-term health benefits of breastfeeding indicates that breastfed babies are less likely than bottle-fed babies to be overweight as children. Research also shows that breastfed babies have a lower incidence and severity of many illnesses including respiratory and urinary tract infections, gastroenteritis, diabetes and childhood cancers.

Research also indicated that there are health benefits for the mothers. Breastfeeding has been found to help prevent breast cancer and reduce the risk of ovarian cancer and diabetes.

DISADVANTAGES OF BREASTFEEDING

* Unless the mother chooses to express the milk, she is solely responsible for all the feedings, which can place an extra workload on her. (However, it does free up her partner for nappy-changing duties!)
* While the mother is breastfeeding, the baby eats whatever she eats, so she must continue to watch her diet, eliminate alcohol and limit intake of caffeine. Some medication should not be taken by breastfeeding mothers: a GP or pharmacist will be able to advise on this.
* The other parent and other relations/friends do not have the chance to bond with the child through bottle-feeding unless the mother expresses the milk using a breast pump.
* A small minority of mothers do not produce enough milk for the baby or may develop sore breasts and find it difficult to breastfeed.

BOTTLE-FEEDING

For the reasons outlined above or because of personal choice, parents may decide to bottle-feed their child with formula milk. There are many different brands available on the market and it may take parents some time to decide which brand best suits their child's needs. Formula milk is designed to meet the child's nutritional requirements.

Vitamin D3

The HSE recommends that babies who are breastfed or predominantly breastfed take a supplement of Vitamin D3. Under Irish law, all formula milk is supplemented by Vitamin D3.

HOW TO MAKE A BOTTLE FEED USING FORMULA

 Key Practical Task

1. Boil fresh tap water in a kettle or covered saucepan. This will kill any bacteria.
2. When the water has boiled, leave it to cool for 30 minutes, **but no longer**. The water should be 70°C.
3. Clean the work surface with disinfectant spray and wash your hands with soap and water.

4. Read the instructions on the label of the formula box to see how much formula powder and water are needed. A general rule of thumb is one scoop of formula powder per fluid ounce (30 ml).

5. Pour the right amount of boiled, cooled water into a sterile bottle (see 'Sterilising feeding equipment', p. 146), measuring the level at the lowest point of the water.

6. Add the exact amount of formula powder, using the scoop provided. Make sure there are no lumps in the mixture and that you only add the exact amount required.

7. Level the scoop off, using either the flat edge of a clean, dry knife or the leveller provided.

8. Screw the bottle lid on tightly, and shake well to mix the contents.

9. Test the temperature of the mix on the inside of your wrist. It should feel lukewarm. The milk should be about 37°C.

10. If it's too hot, hold the bottle under cold running water or place it in a large bowl of cold water. Make sure that the cold water does not reach above the neck of the bottle.

11. Dry the outside of the bottle with a clean cloth.

12. Feed the baby.

Warning!

If you have a water softener system in place for your tap water, you should not use the tap water to make a bottle, as it may be too high in sodium.

Do not use bottled water labelled as 'natural mineral water', as this can also be high in sodium.

  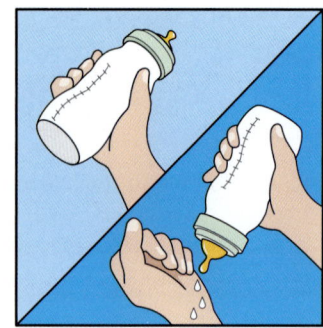

Preparing a formula feed

HOW TO BOTTLE-FEED A CHILD

 Key Practical Task

1. Having prepared the feed, sit down with the child in your arms. Never prop or lean the bottle against a cushion or other support, as this can cause the baby to choke.
2. Have a muslin cloth to hand for winding the child to protect your clothes in the event of posseting.
3. Stimulate the rooting reflex by placing the teat in the corner of the child's mouth. The child will then open their mouth and you can place the teat of the bottle fully in the mouth.
4. Tilt the bottle so that the hole in the teat is always covered with milk.
5. Keep the teat full of milk so that the baby is not swallowing air.
6. Talk to the baby throughout as you give the feed. Eye contact is really important during the feed, as it helps to build the bond of attachment between the adult and baby.
7. Sit or hold the baby upright and rub or pat their back to bring up any wind.
8. Follow the lead of the baby: take it slowly and do not rush them to finish. Never force a baby to finish a full feed.
9. If the baby does not finish the feed, throw away any feed the baby has not taken after two hours.

Top Tips!

* Prepare formula feed as required to prevent bacteria growth.
* Any unused feed should be thrown away after 24 hours.
* When making the formula feed, be careful not to compress the formula powder or to use lumpy powder, as this can lead to the feed becoming over-concentrated. This can cause constipation and dehydration.
* Equally, make sure that the scoop is filled to the top and that there are no air pockets to ensure that you are adding the correct amount of formula powder.

STORAGE OF FORMULA FEED

Parents may choose to make up bottles of formula milk in batches instead of making a fresh feed on demand. Pre-made bottles of formula milk can be stored in a fridge for 24 hours. When heating a bottle, sit the bottle in a jug of warm water for 15 minutes. Never use a microwave to re-heat feeds: microwaves heat unevenly, and this can cause hot spots, which can scald the baby's mouth.

Packets of pre-made formula feed are also available and are useful when going on journeys with children. Parents whose children are still using bottles should bring a supply of pre-made formula milk in a cool bag to the setting each day. The bottles must then be placed in the fridge and labelled so that the right feed goes to the right child.

STERILISING FEEDING EQUIPMENT

 **Key Practical Task**

Feeding equipment for babies up to 1 year old must be sterilised. Sterilisation removes harmful bacteria that a baby's developing immune system cannot yet deal with. Before sterilising, wash all bottles, teats and covers in warm soapy water, using a bottle brush, to remove any milk residue. This should be done as soon after feeding as possible to prevent bacteria from multiplying. Three methods of sterilisation can be used.

Steam sterilising is a fast and efficient way of sterilising. The bottles, teats and caps are placed in the steam steriliser, following the manufacturer's instructions. Steam sterilising usually takes about ten minutes and is relatively hassle free.

1. Steam sterilising

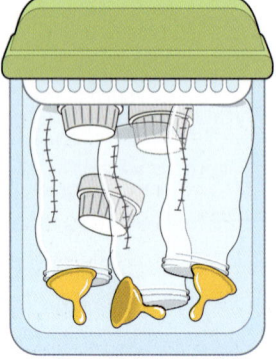

2. Chemical sterilising

Cold water chemical sterilising involves immersing the feeding equipment in a diluted disinfectant such as Milton. Chemical sterilisation usually takes about 15 to 30 minutes.

Although not commonplace in ELC settings for health and safety reasons, boiling is another method of sterilisation. Immerse the feeding equipment in a large saucepan half-filled with cold water, cover the pan, bring to the boil and boil for at least three minutes.

3. Boiling

> ### Note
> Whichever method you use, you must be careful when removing the now sterile feeding equipment. **Do not** touch the equipment with your bare hands; use tongs to remove it. Never touch the teat of the bottle with your hands; use sterile tongs.

Feeding Issues

During a baby's first year they may experience wind, colic or reflux.

WIND

Wind is the name given to air that the baby has swallowed while feeding, usually when feeding, crying or yawning. It commonly occurs when the baby has fed too fast or too slowly. The trapped air causes the baby to feel uncomfortable or full and to cry, squirm or stop feeding. It is very common from the newborn stage until about 3 months. Wind is a normal part of feeding and is easily treated by 'winding' the baby. At the end of the feed, place the baby over your shoulder or across your lap and pat or rub their back gently to help the baby to burp and relieve the trapped wind. You may need to put a towel on your shoulder to protect your clothes as sometimes the baby brings up small amounts of milk while being winded. This is called posseting.

COLIC

Babies with colic have spells of non-stop inconsolable crying and irritability. Colic affects both breastfed and bottle-fed babies. It is not known exactly what causes colic, but it is thought to be related to a build-up of wind, overstimulation or gut contractions caused by lactose intolerance. Colic is a common problem and affects one in five babies. Most babies outgrow colic between 4 and 6 months. Parents can take steps to reduce colic by rocking the baby, baby massage, reducing wind by using special bottles, sitting the baby upright during feeds and not changing breasts too quickly when breastfeeding. Some parents find music, movement and 'white noise' like the noise of a dishwasher or washing machine can help. You can even find videos of white noise for colicky babies on YouTube!

REFLUX

Reflux occurs when small quantities of milk are vomited up soon after feeding. Reflux affects up to 40 per cent of babies. Most babies grow out of reflux, and it is usually not serious if the baby is gaining weight and otherwise well. It usually occurs because the baby's oesophagus (food pipe) is still developing.

Signs and symptom of reflux include:

* spitting up milk during or after feeds
* refusing feeds, gagging or choking
* persistent hiccups or coughing
* excessive crying or crying when feeding
* frequent ear infections.

Reflux can be managed by reducing the volume of feeds, avoiding moving the baby straight after a feed and winding the baby. However, if the reflux is persistent or excessive, further measures may be needed. The GP or Public Health Nurse will advise parents on options, which may include using a thickened formula.

If a child in your care shows signs of reflux, record the time and a description of the reflux and notify the parents at the end of the day.

Drinks for babies

DRINKS FOR BABIES UNDER 6 MONTHS

Breastfed babies do not need any other drinks than breast milk. If babies are being fed with formula, this can be supplemented with cooled boiled water. This can help with constipation.

DRINKS FOR BABIES AGED 6 TO 12 MONTHS

From 6 months onwards, the parent will start to introduce the child to using a cup to drink. Babies should be weaned off the bottle and should only be using a cup by their first birthday. Cooled boiled tap water can continue to be given to the baby. Babies should not be given fizzy drinks, fruit juice, or tea or coffee.

Weaning

'Weaning' is the term given to the gradual introduction of solid foods into the baby's diet. For the first few months of a baby's life, the baby gets all the nutrients they need from breast milk or formula feeds. However, as the baby grows, they need a more varied diet. This usually happens between 4 and 6 months. Bottle-fed babies will need to be weaned earlier than breastfed babies. It is important not to wean babies any earlier than 4 months, as their digestive system is still maturing and is not able to process solid foods. Babies should not be weaned any later than 6 months: if weaning is left any later, children may be reluctant to start eating solids.

Signs a baby is ready for solid foods include:

* they are able to sit up with support and can control their head movements
* they can look at food, pick it up and put it in their mouth by themselves
* they can swallow food instead of spitting it back out.

Chewing fists, waking in the night and wanting extra milk feeds are **not signs** that the baby is ready to be weaned.

BEGINNING TO WEAN

Before weaning can begin, the parents will need a baby bowl and spoon, steriliser and liquidiser or blender. New foods should be introduced one at a time, starting with small amounts (one tablespoon) and gradually building up to larger amounts.

The first foods should be smooth, with no lumps, such as puréed carrot. Breast milk/formula milk or cooled boiled water can be added to get the purée to the right consistency. Some parents make their own food, others purchase processed baby food. If a parent makes their own food, they can control the salt, sugar and additives. Homemade food will also taste better and be more varied for the baby.

It is best to start weaning in the afternoon, when the baby is most alert. There are three stages in weaning, as shown in the following table.

Stage	Food	Consistency	Drink	Foods not to be given
Stage 1 (4–6 months)	Puréed meat, peas and beans Puréed fruit/vegetables Puréed potatoes Gluten-free cereals, e.g. baby rice	Food should be puréed and of a soft consistency with no lumps	Breastmilk or formula feed Cooled boiled water	Any food containing gluten Nuts Eggs Cow's milk
Stage 2 (6-9 months)	Well-cooked eggs Porridge/Ready Brek Bread, rice and pasta Cheese	Thicker purée Minced Mashed Finely chopped	Breastmilk or formula feed Cooled boiled water	Nuts Unpasteurized cheese Eggs
Stage 3 (9-12 months)	A variety of food can be given	Lumpy foods Chopped and mashed Harder finger foods Wide variety of foods and texture	As for Stage 2	As for Stage 2

FINGER FOODS

As children's fine motor skills develop, they should be encouraged to self-feed using finger foods – foods that are easily picked up in the pincer grasp. This can take place when the baby is aged between 7 and 9 months.

Examples of finger food include:

* cheese slices or cubes
* ripe peeled fruit
* cooked, soft vegetables
* buttered toast (without the crust).

Self-feeding should be encouraged as much as possible. It can be messy, but it is a vital social skill the baby must master and helps to develop their independence and autonomy. Never rush the child or put them under pressure to 'eat faster'.

Once weaning has been completed, the child will need to take in adequate food for their day-to-day requirements.

FOODS TO AVOID GIVING BABIES

* Salt is toxic to babies because their kidneys cannot process it properly. It should never be added to babies' food.
* Nuts should not be given to children under 5, as they are a choking hazard.
* Whole eggs should not be given to babies under 8 months.
* Do not give spinach, turnip or beetroot to a baby under 6 months.
* Cow's milk should be avoided until the baby is 1 year old, but it can be used to soften food.

Key Practical Task

When spoon feeding a baby, make sure to follow these steps:

1. Wash the baby's hands before mealtime begins
2. Spoon feed the baby when they are fully alert and sitting up strapped into their highchair
3. Offer the baby a spoon of food at a time. As the baby gets older you should encourage them to feed themselves. Don't worry if they make a mess- this is part of how they learn.
4. From the time the baby is seven months, offer the baby finger foods which they can feed themselves.
5. Do not rush the baby, mealtimes should be a relaxing experience.
6. Talk and chat to the baby while you are feeding them.

Nutrition for Toddlers and Young Children

13

After reading this chapter you will:
* discuss the food pyramid
* plan nutritious, well-balanced meals for the children in your care
* accommodate any special dietary requirements the children in your care may have
* promote healthy eating in the ELC setting.

 Key Practical Task

This chapter covers the following key practical task:
* Mealtimes for toddlers and young children.

Children need the right nutrition to grow healthy and strong. This chapter will teach you about healthy eating for children. If you are interested in learning more about nutrition, read *The Book of Nutrition* (McMahon, 2021).

The Food Pyramid

The food pyramid is a visual guide to a healthy diet and is designed to illustrate how to plan a balanced diet. There are two versions of the food pyramid: one for children aged 1 to 4, and one for those over the age of 4 years.

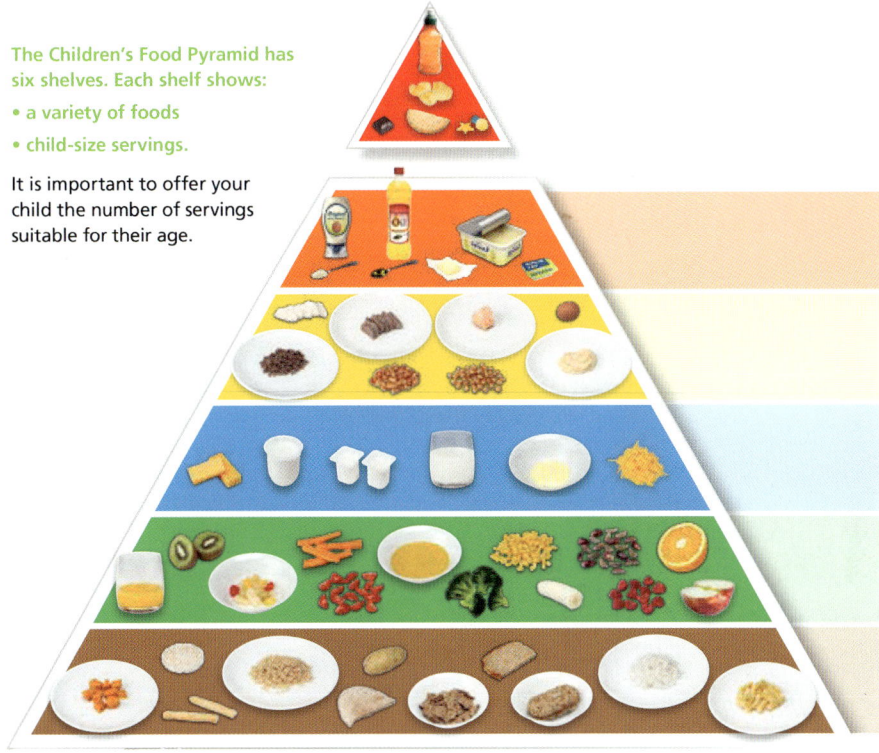

Each type of food is represented by a group on the pyramid, with a recommendation for the number of portions of that food per day. As you can see, groups 1 and 2 are reversed on the child food pyramid. This is because very young children need carbohydrates to fuel their healthy growth.

GROUP 1: WHOLEMEAL CEREALS AND BREADS, POTATOES, PASTA AND RICE

The foods in this group provide our main energy source. Children aged 1 to 4, teenage boys and active men aged 18 to 50 need more servings from this group. When choosing food options from this group, wholemeal options are preferred. However, this should be limited in the case of very young children, as wholemeal options are higher in fibre, which can cause constipation.

GROUP 2: VEGETABLES, SALADS AND FRUIT

This group is really important for providing the body with essential vitamins and minerals, and it is also a source of fibre. This is the biggest group for adults, so vegetables, fruit and salad should form the basis of the adult diet. Fruit juice and fruit-based smoothies should be limited, as the process of juicing removes most of the fibre.

GROUP 3: MILK, YOGURT AND CHEESE

Dairy products are essential for young children, as they are high in calcium, which is needed for healthy bones and teeth. Plant-based substitutes, such as almond milk, coconut milk and rice milk, are not suitable for young children as they contain little or no calcium. If a child needs a non-dairy alternative, they should drink soya milk fortified with calcium. Low-fat and fat-free milk are not suitable for children under the age of 2. Children need three portions of milk and dairy products daily, but for children between 9 and 18, this increases to five portions daily.

GROUP 4: MEAT, POULTRY, FISH, EGGS, BEANS AND NUTS

This group provides us with our protein intake and is needed for healthy growth. Processed meats are high in salt and saturated fat and should be eaten in moderation. Fish should be eaten twice a week, as it is an important source of omega-3 fatty acid.

GROUP 5: FATS, SPREADS AND OILS

Foods in this group include butter, margarine and vegetable oil. Children and adults should limit their intake of this group to two servings daily.

GROUP 6: FOODS HIGH IN FATS, SALT AND SUGAR

This group includes biscuits, chocolate, sweets and crisps. Intake of the foods in this group needs to be restricted: they should not be consumed every day. Very small amounts once or twice a week is sufficient.

Legislation

Under Regulation 22 of the Early Years Services Regulations 2016, all ELC settings must ensure that adequate, suitable varied and nutritious food is provided for all children. Some ELC settings provide food; others require parents to send food in with children.

Food and Nutrition Guidelines for Pre-School Services

In 2004, the Department of Health and Children published guidelines on the provision of food in pre-school services (DoHC, 2004). The guidelines set out the requirements for the provision of meals in an ELC setting and are used by the Tusla Inspection teams to assess the provision of food and nutrition in all such settings. It is recommended that food should be offered to young children at least every three hours.

* **Children in full day care (more than five hours):** Offer at least two meals and two snacks, for example breakfast, snack, lunch and snack. One meal should be a hot

meal. If children are there for a long day, an evening meal may also need to be provided. If a main meal is not provided for some reason, ensure that parents know this so they can offer suitable meals at home.

* **Children in day care for up to five hours per session:** Offer at least two meals and one snack, for example breakfast, snack and lunch. It is not necessary to serve a hot meal, but the meal should include at least one serving from each of the four main shelves of the food pyramid.

* **Children in day care for up to 3.5 hours per session:** Offer one meal and one snack, for example snack and lunch. This group may also include afterschool care.

The HSE published '3-Week Menu Plan: A Resource for Pre-schools', which supports pre-schools in planning meals to implement the 2004 guidelines.

PORTION SIZE

The Department of Health published 'Healthy eating for 1- to 4-year-olds: The Children's Food Pyramid Guidelines', which contains a portion size guide for pre-schools, with very useful images of how big each portion size should be.

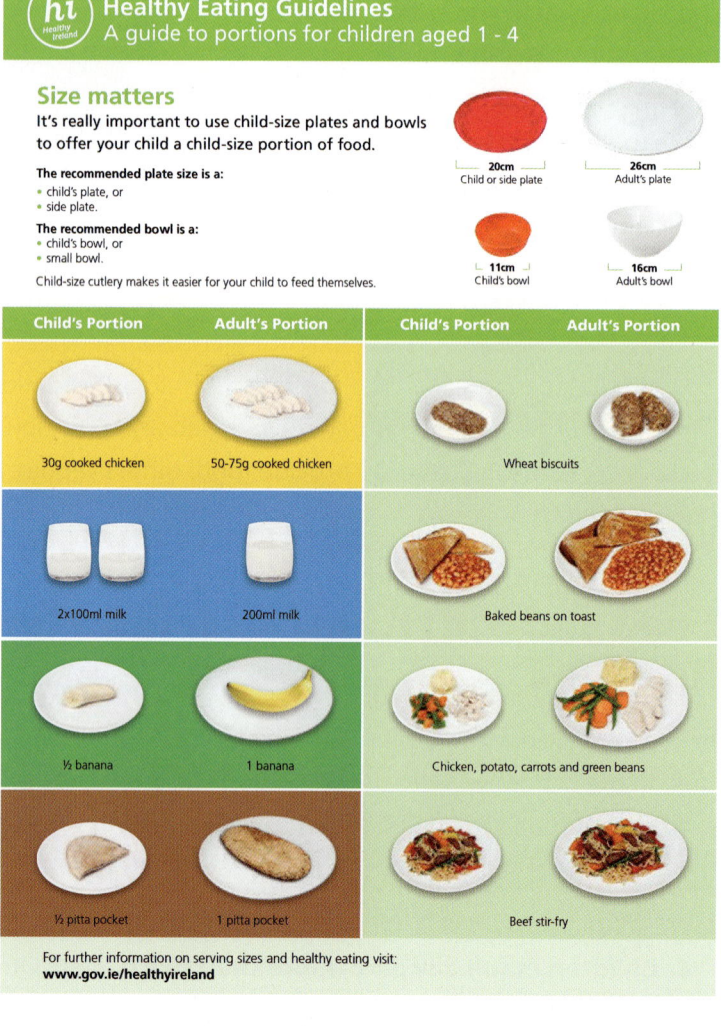

FLUID INTAKE

Water is essential for life; humans can survive for up to eight weeks without food but only a few days without water. The body loses water daily though sweat, the excretion of urine and from chemical reactions in the body cells. An adult should take in two to three litres of water daily, at least two litres of which should come from beverages – the rest comes from our food.

SOME FUNCTIONS OF WATER

* Water is vital to life – the body is 60 per cent water while the brain is 78 per cent water (McMahon, 2021).
* Water transports nutrients, oxygen, hormones and enzymes around the body.
* Water transports waste products and carbon dioxide around the body.
* Water helps to regulate temperature and keep the body cool.

When planning a healthy diet for children we must also consider their fluid intake. The HSE 2004 guidelines also cover the provision of drinks and fluids. Water should be readily available throughout the day and children should be encouraged to drink up to six cups of fluid per day. Water for infants under 12 months should be boiled and cooled before use. Note that bottled water is not suitable for infants under 12 months, as it can contain high levels of sodium.

Water intake must be increased when the child is ill (for example vomiting or diarrhoea) or after intense physical activity. Water intake must also be increased in hot weather, as the body sweats more. If fluid intake is not increased at these times dehydration can result.

DEHYDRATION

Dehydration can occur after a 2 per cent loss of water. Signs of dehydration include:

* headaches
* muscle cramps
* feeling dizzy and lightheaded
* having a dry or sticky mouth
* producing less urine and darker urine
* negative mood.

Note: Feeling thirsty is not an early warning sign.

Signs of extreme dehydration include:

* not producing urine
* sleepiness
* sunken eyes
* sunken fontanelle in babies
* fainting.

DEHYDRATION IN CHILDREN

If a child in your care shows any of the following symptoms of dehydration, you must summon medical assistance:

* not producing tears/dry eyes
* sunken eyes
* little or no urine output for eight hours
* dry skin that sags back into position slowly when pinched up into a fold
* dry mouth
* sunken soft spot on the top of an infant's head
* fast-beating heart
* blood in the stools or vomit
* diarrhoea or vomiting (in infants under 2 months old)
* listlessness and inactivity.

WHAT DRINKS SHOULD BE OFFERED TO CHILDREN?

Young babies should be given breast milk/formula milk. Cooled boiled water may be given if the baby is thirsty. This water should be taken from the tap: bottled water should not be used because some bottled water contains high levels of sodium, which is poisonous to babies. Babies can be given full-fat cow's milk after their first birthday. Do not give babies low-fat or skimmed milk, as they need the essential fat-soluble vitamins that are found in full-fat milk.

Juice is high in sugar, so it should not be given to babies under 6 months, and only sparingly after that. Unsweetened juice can be given to children, but only with meals to limit the potential damage to their teeth.

Tea and coffee are **not suitable** for young children, as they contain high levels of caffeine and tannin, a substance which interferes with iron absorption. Fizzy drinks, such as cola and lemonade, are acidic and high in sugar and **should not be given to young children**.

Impact of a Poor Diet on Children

Early childhood is a time of extraordinary growth and development. An unbalanced diet or one that fails to meet nutritional guidelines in early childhood can have a negative impact on children's health and well-being.

DELAYED GROWTH

Young children need to eat sufficient calories from high-quality foods. If this does not happen, it can lead to delayed growth and the child being under height for their age. According to UNICEF (United Nations Children's Emergency Fund), 149 million children around the world have stunted growth, or are too short for their age, because of malnutrition (UNICEF, 2019).

DENTAL PROBLEMS

A diet high in sugar can cause dental cavities in children and adults. Children and adults should follow good oral hygiene. Drinks that are high in sugar, such as fizzy drinks and fruit juice, should be avoided.

OBESITY

Children whose diet is too high in calories may experience obesity. A child is considered overweight if they weigh 10 to 20 per cent over the ideal weight for their age and height.

A child is considered obese if they weigh 20 per cent or more over the ideal weight for their age and height. The 'National Pre-School Nutrition Survey' (Walton, 2012) found that one in four Irish pre-schoolers were overweight or obese. More recently, a survey found that one in five Irish primary school children is obese (Mitchell et al., 2020).

DIFFICULTY WITH MEMORY AND CONCENTRATION

There is some evidence that children who eat a poor diet experience difficulties with memory and concentration, especially in school. There is evidence that children and teenagers who have low iron levels may not perform as well in school as those with no iron issues (Taras, 2005), and there is some evidence that iron deficiency may be associated with higher levels of behavioural problems in children (Corapci et al., 2010; Lozoff et al., 1998).

SLEEP ISSUES

Children who have a diet high in sugary drinks and foods may have difficulty getting to sleep at night-time. As you learned in Chapter 8, children need a lot of sleep; it is essential for their developing brain. Poor sleep may cause the child to be irritable in the ELC setting.

Linking *Síolta* and *Aistear* to nutrition for the ELC setting

Standard 9.4 of *Síolta* states that a quality ELC setting is 'proactive in supporting the development of healthy eating habits in children whilst supporting their enjoyment and appreciation of eating as a positive social experience' (DES, 2017, p. 66).

The *Aistear* Theme of Well-being, Aim 2, Learning Goal 6 states that children will 'make healthy choices and demonstrate positive attitudes to nutrition, hygiene, exercise and routine' (NCCA, 2009, p. 6)

Both *Síolta* and *Aistear*, therefore, require the ELC setting and ELC practitioner to support young children in making nutritious food choices.

Role of the ELC Practitioner in Supporting Children's Nutrition

ELC practitioners have an important role in supporting children's nutrition, as shown in the below diagram.

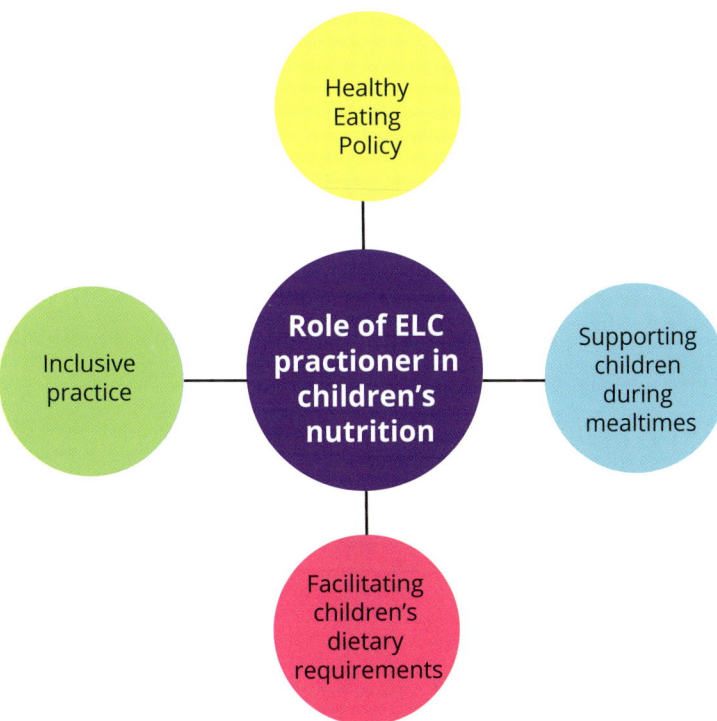

HEALTHY EATING POLICY

Under the Early Years Services Regulations 2016, every ELC setting must have a healthy eating policy. This must be shared with and explained to parents. It should include:

* the fact that suitable and nutritious food is available to all children
* the menu you use in your service, and information about how it is communicated to parents/guardians
* a note about how changes to the menu are handled
* information about how the choices of parents/guardians are supported
* an outline of how it will be communicated to parents/guardians when their child has not eaten well
* details of how infant formula milk powder is managed

- details of how food is safely stored and prepared
- information about how specific dietary requirements are catered for.

> **Look it up**
>
> Read the Healthy Eating policy which is in operation in your professional placement setting.

SUPPORTING CHILDREN DURING MEALTIMES

Meal and snack times in the ELC setting should be treated as a social occasion. Get the children involved in the routine and ask them to help to set up the table with tablecloths, place mats and cutlery. The ELC practitioner should sit with children during meal and snack times. Encourage children to self-feed, but you can give support to younger children who may need assistance. It is good practice if the ELC practitioner eats with the children to model good eating habits and to further support the routine of mealtime.

Mealtimes should never be rushed. Some children will eat quickly, others more slowly. Never rush a child or tell them to 'eat faster'.

FOOD REFUSAL

Food refusal is a repeated refusal to eat, chew or swallow food. Food refusal can be common in toddlers, who may be too busy having fun and exploring the world to eat! Food refusal is also one of the ways toddlers express their independence and personality – remember, it is during the toddler years that the child starts to say, 'No!' Food refusal can also be because of the child engaging in unhealthy feeding habits that affect their appetite. These can include as follows:

- Drinking too much juice/soft drinks/diluted drinks. If toddlers consume more than two glasses of these drinks a day, it will fill up their stomach and thus reduce their appetite.
- Drinking too much formula milk will also affect a child's appetite.
- A child who is given too many treat foods or who is 'grazing' and snacking continually throughout the day may not be hungry at mealtimes.

Many children will occasionally have 'off days' when they do not eat well. However, if the child has been eating poorly for several days and is not unwell, it may be a case of food refusal. Several steps can be taken to deal with food refusal.

* Make a list of everything the child is eating and drinking during the day. If the child is drinking a lot of fluids or eating a lot of treat foods, discuss with the parent.
* Check when the child is eating. It may be that the child is grazing during the day and is simply not hungry at mealtimes. If this is the case, stop the grazing and standardise mealtimes. Mealtimes should be regular and familiar: children thrive on routine!
* Make mealtimes an occasion free from distractions. Children learn by watching others, especially their parents and siblings. If the family eats together, the child will be more likely to want to eat with their family. In the ELC setting, the ELC practitioner should eat with the children to model good eating behaviour.
* Never bribe or force a child to eat.

FACTORS THAT INFLUENCE FOOD INTAKE

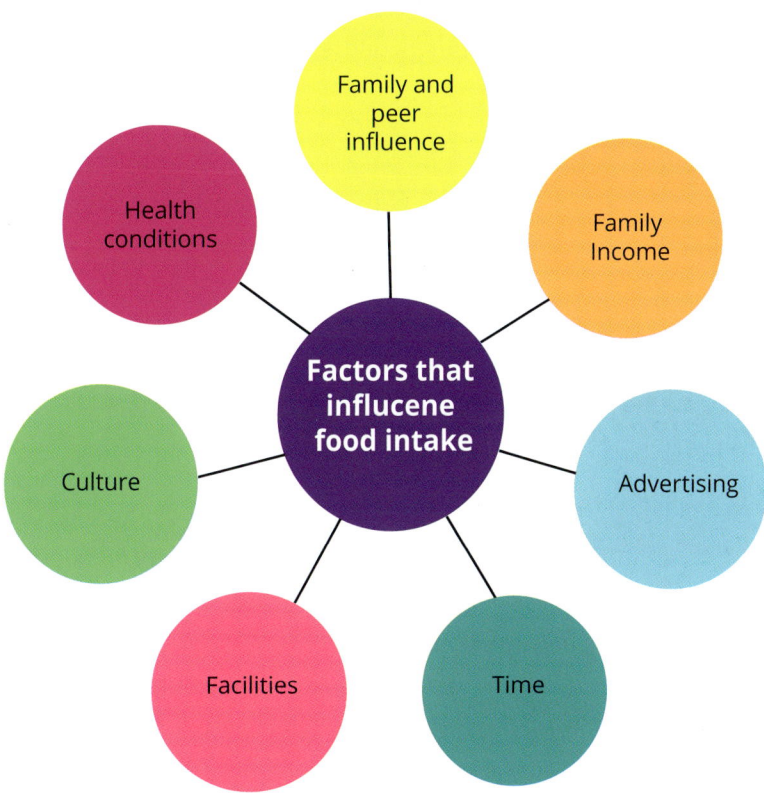

FAMILY AND PEER INFLUENCE

The family has responsibility for choosing what their child eats. Therefore families should try to provide children with a wide range of healthy options to encourage them to develop good eating habits. As children get older, they may imitate the eating habits of their peers. This can be a positive or a negative factor. Children may be encouraged to try food which they see their peers eating. On the other hand, they may be turned off those foods that they hear their peers describe as 'yucky'.

FAMILY INCOME
Income is closely linked to food choice. Food poverty is defined as the 'inability to afford or have reasonable access to food which provides a healthy diet' (Farrell *et al.*, 2008, p. 53). The organisation Safefood estimates that food can account for up to one-third of the take-home income of a lower income household (Safefood, 2019) and that 10 per cent of households in Ireland experience food poverty.

ADVERTISING
Advertisers use celebrities and advertising campaigns to make certain food appealing to consumers. They also may use promotions, such as free gifts. Unfortunately, these foods may not always be the healthy options. For example, McDonald's use advertising and the free toy with a Happy Meal to target young children.

TIME
Many families are time poor. Busy working parents may find it difficult to allocate time to cooking healthy meals and instead rely on convenience foods. Batch cooking on a Sunday is one way to tackle this problem.

FACILITIES
Some families live in situations where they do not have adequate facilities for cooking. For example, families experiencing homelessness and those living in direct provision may not have access to cooking facilities.

CULTURE
Food is a big part of an individual's cultural identity. A child's cultural background may influence the type of food they eat at home. For example, a child from a Polish background may eat *pierogi*, a type of dumpling. A child from a Nigerian background may eat yam, a type of vegetable. However, be careful not to stereotype and make assumptions about a child's food preferences because of their cultural background. As always, if in doubt, check with the parents.

HEALTH CONDITIONS
Some children in your care will have specific dietary requirements for health reasons. Some health conditions that require special diets include food allergies such as coeliac condition, diabetes, cystic fibrosis, PKU, galactosaemia and lactose intolerance.

FACILITATING CHILDREN'S DIETARY REQUIREMENTS

FOOD ALLERGIES

A food allergy is an abnormal response of the immune system to an otherwise harmless food. According to the Irish Nutrition and Dietetic Institute (www.indi.ie), up to five per cent of children and three per cent of adults have food allergies. The most common food allergies are to:

* peanuts
* soya
* tree nuts, such as almonds and walnuts
* wheat
* milk
* shellfish
* eggs
* fish.

Allergic reactions range in severity. The most common symptoms of an allergic reaction include itchy skin, hives, nausea, sore eyes and feeling faint. The most severe allergic reaction is known as anaphylaxis, which affects several areas of the body. Anaphylactic shock results in a raised pulse rate and impaired breathing and can be fatal.

The role of the ELC practitioner in caring for a child with allergies

If a child who attends the ELC setting has a severe food allergy, this food should be excluded from the setting. For example, if a child has a severe nut allergy, the setting should implement a 'no nut' policy. A personalised allergy/intolerance management plan must be developed for the child and all staff made aware of the plan. It is useful to have this on a chart in the room with a picture of the child. When preparing food take care to avoid cross-contamination with the allergen. Parents/guardians should provide an up-to-date emergency plan in case of a reaction. Depending on the severity of the child's allergy this may involve providing staff with adrenaline autoinjectors, such as an EpiPen, or relieving medication. Practitioners should be trained in how to administer the autoinjector if needed.

Emergency medical treatment should be sought at once if you suspect anaphylactic shock. A child with an allergy may have an adrenaline pen, and if the child goes into anaphylactic shock this must be administered immediately.

COELIAC CONDITION

Coeliac condition means a person's intestine has an abnormal response to gluten, a protein found in wheat, oats, rye and barley. If a person who has coeliac condition eats gluten they will damage their small intestine, as the body mistakenly perceives gluten as the enemy and attacks it. This causes the small intestine to become inflamed and unable to absorb nutrients properly. Symptoms typical of coeliac disease are diarrhoea, constipation, weight loss, pot belly, mouth ulcers, fatigue, indigestion and stomach bloating. It is not known what causes coeliac disease.

The role of the ELC practitioner in caring for a child with coeliac condition

You must ensure that there are gluten-free alternatives available for the child. The child will not be able to eat wheat, so you will have to plan a wheat-free diet. Be aware that many processed foods, such as sausages and burgers, contain gluten and check whether the ones you are providing contain gluten. The Coeliac Society of Ireland maintains an up-to-date list of coeliac-friendly products. Further information is available at www.coeliac.ie. Be aware of the risk of cross-contamination when gluten-free foods come into contact with foods containing gluten. Different kitchen utensils must be used when preparing gluten-free food and food containing gluten.

LACTOSE INTOLERANCE

This is the inability to absorb lactose, which is the main sugar found in milk. It is common in young children, as the enzyme the body uses to break down lactose has not yet matured, and often occurs in premature babies. The symptoms of lactose intolerance, which usually occur between 30 minutes and two hours after eating, include:

* wind
* stomach rumbling
* diarrhoea
* floating or foul-smelling stools
* nausea

* weight loss
* a bloated feeling.

Role of the ELC practitioner in caring for a child with lactose intolerance

A dietician will devise a suitable diet in consultation with other healthcare professionals and parents. ELC practitioners will need to follow the dietary requirements as laid out by the dietician and parents.

Partnership with parents

It is really important that you work closely with the parents of any children who require special diet and that you follow the guidelines the parents give you.

INCLUSIVE PRACTICE

Food is an important part of cultural identity for both children and adults. It is important that the ELC setting reflects and respects this.

Additionally, the requirement to adhere to a certain diet and abstain from certain foods or to fast at certain times of the year is a feature of many world religions. It is the responsibility of the ELC practitioner to find out if this affects any of the children in their care and to make adequate provision for these children.

ISLAM

Muslim children are required to abstain from pork and pork products, any fish without scales and any meat that is not killed in the way laid down by the Qur'an (the holy book of Islam). This includes certain jellies that are made using gelatine. All children are to be breastfed until age two. Fasting is observed during the lunar month of Ramadan. During this time Muslims abstain from all food and drink between sunrise and sunset. Children under 12 years are exempt from observing Ramadan.

JUDAISM

Animals and birds must be slaughtered in accordance with Jewish law to be kosher (acceptable). Pork and shellfish are forbidden. Milk and meat must not be cooked or eaten together.

HINDUISM

Orthodox Hindus are vegetarians because they believe in *ahimsa* – non-violence towards living things. Non-orthodox Hindus will not eat beef, because the cow is considered a sacred animal; or pork, because the pig is considered unclean.

> ### Further reading
> *The Book of Nutrition* (McMahon, 2021) gives a comprehensive overview of nutritional needs of children and adults.

Section 7

Physical Activity

Active Play and Physical Exercise

After reading this chapter you will:

* understand the importance of active play in early childhood
* understand the importance of fundamental movement skills (FMS)
* be able to plan and organise activities to encourage children to be active
* be able to plan inclusive physical activity opportunities for children.

Key Term

Fundamental movement skills (FMS): These are the basic physical movements that children need to learn in childhood that set the foundations for activity and exercise in later childhood and adulthood.

Active Play

Active play is the name given to any activity that encourages children to move and have fun. It is essential for physical and emotional well-being. Active play can be made up of:

1. everyday tasks, such as climbing steps, helping to tidy up
2. unstructured activities that have no rules, such as dancing, chasing, skipping
3. structured activities that have rules, including kicking a ball, playing games like chase and hide-and-seek, organised sports
4. active travel, for example walking, pedalling or scooting to get from one place to another.

(HSE)

Daily active play is essential to help children to:

1. develop their senses
2. develop strength
3. learn about their bodies
4. build social and emotional bonds with each other
5. develop fundamental movement skills.

When children engage in active play, they develop their senses of touch and sight. They explore the texture of different items, whether that is natural materials such as leaves and stones, or human-made toys such as different textured balls. They will develop strength in their muscles and bones, for example, as they throw, kick or catch a ball, or in music and movement where they strengthen their arms and legs. Active play helps children to learn about their bodies. For example, they learn that when they run fast, they breath faster. ELC practitioners can use this as a discussion point for children about how our bodies work. In active play children build social and emotional bonds with each other: play is how children develop friendships. Finally, active play is essential for developing children's fundamental movement skills, the basic movements needed for physical activity.

Role of the ELC practitioner to encourage active play in the ELC setting

As you are aware, children imitate and model themselves on high-status role models such as ELC practitioners. As such, ELC practitioners should act as positive role models and encourage active play and physical activity in children. Get up and be active: the children will imitate this! It is important to be enthusiastic and energetic when modelling active play for young children.

CASE STUDY: ELC PRACTITIONER AS A ROLE MODEL FOR ACTIVE PLAY

Tomasz and Jane both work in the ECCE room of a large ELC setting. They have different attitudes to active play and exercise. Tomasz strongly believes that children should be encouraged to be active. He loves being outdoors and gets the children outside as much as possible. If it is raining, sometimes he asks the children to wrap up and go outside anyway so they can play in the puddles. Tomasz believes that there is no such thing as bad weather – only inappropriate clothes!

Jane has a different attitude. She prefers to be inside and hates being cold and wet. When they are outside, Jane gets worried that the children will fall and hurt themselves. She said this to Tomasz, but Tomasz just laughed and said, 'Children fall; it's a normal part of childhood. Don't worry: I have the first aid box in case of an accident.'

Today, when it was time for outdoor play, the sky was overcast. Before Tomasz could say anything, Jane said, 'Oh, what a pity – it looks like it will rain. Let's do arts and crafts instead.' Tomasz was cross about this, but felt he couldn't say anything in front of the children.

Question

When you read this story, do you identify more with Tomasz or Jane? Reflect on this. Think about what your own attitude to active play is and how this might influence the children in your care.

HOW ACTIVE SHOULD CHILDREN BE?

The HSE recommends that children over the age of 3 should be physically active for at least three hours spread across the day. At least one hour of this should be structured activities, such as playing chase or football. This should include vigorous activity, moderate activity, muscle-strengthening and bone-strengthening exercise

Exercise category	Definition	Examples
Vigorous activity	Activity that causes the heart to beat much faster than normal and breathing to be much harder than normal	Games of chase and running Skipping rope Games like soccer, Gaelic football, rugby
Moderate activity	Activity that causes the heart to beat faster than normal and breathing to be harder than normal	Walking Bicycle riding

Exercise category	Definition	Examples
Muscle strengthening	Exercise that helps to strengthen children's muscles	Tug of war
		Playing on playground equipment
		Yoga
		Stretching
Bone strengthening	Exercises that help to strengthen children's bones	Hopscotch
		Gymnastics
		Skipping
		Running

(Source: DoHC, HSE, 2009)

HOW ACTIVE ARE IRISH CHILDREN?

Research indicates that Irish children do not currently get enough exercise. The 'Children's Sport Participation and Physical Activity' study was carried out by Sports Ireland in 2018. It found that only 17 per cent of primary children and 10 per cent of post-primary children meet the National Physical Activity Guidelines. It also found that, on average, primary school children spend **five hours of their leisure time in sedentary activity per day**. For post-primary children this rose to **seven hours of sedentary activity**.

Fundamental Movement Skills (FMS)

ELC practitioners can help children to stay active throughout their childhood by creating conditions to help develop their fundamental movement skills (FMS). FMS are basic physical movements that children need to learn in childhood that set the foundations for activity and exercise in later childhood and adulthood. Fundamental movement skills support children's overall development, especially their co-ordination and physical dexterity (NCCA, 2015). They provide the building blocks for more advanced movements used by children as they become involved in and enjoy a range of different physical activities. Research shows a positive association between acquisition of FMS and lifelong physical activity: in other words, children who master FMS in early childhood are much more likely to be active for life. There are three categories of FMS, as shown in the following table.

Locomotor skills	Balance skills	Manipulation skills
Crawling	Climbing	Throwing a ball
Walking	Bending	Catching a ball
Running	Rolling	Kicking a ball
Galloping	Turning	Bouncing a ball
Skipping	Stretching	Dribbling a ball
Jumping	Twisting	Two-hand striking with a bat

Despite the importance of FMS, Irish children are not developing them fully. A study of Irish primary school children found that most children scored poorly in FMS (Behan *et al.*, 2019). Forty per cent of children showed a poor mastery of balance skills and just under fifty per cent showed poor levels of locomotor and manipulation skills. Fundamental movement skills can be learned and developed. Therefore, ELC practitioners need to be aware of FMS and help children to develop them. We can help children develop their FMS in the following ways.

ENRICHING ENVIRONMENT

An enriching environment is essential for children to develop their FMS. Standard 2 of *Síolta* (NCCA, 2017) states that both indoor and outdoor ELC environments should be developmentally appropriate and provide 'challenging and stimulating experiences' (p. 19). This means providing the space and material to encourage children to move, run, skip and play. Children's activity levels have been found to increase as more time is spent outside, so ELC settings should facilitate children to spend as much time outside as they can.

CHILD-INITIATED PLAY

Child-initiated play is play that is freely chosen and directed by the child. When given the time and space, children will engage in physical play that tests their physical activity. As the adult, you need to step back, follow the child's lead and give them the freedom to explore their physical capabilities.

TIME

Children need time to wallow and engage in child-initiated play within the enabling environment. Give children time to play and to test their physical abilities. When we rush children, they are less likely to push their physical limits and take risks.

RISKY PLAY

It is important to facilitate children to engage in risky play. Risky play for pre-school children could involve balancing on a beam, climbing or jumping. When we expose children to age-appropriate risky play they learn how to manage risk and develop a sense of autonomy. It also allows them to test their physical movements and to develop their FMS.

PLAYFUL ADULT-LED ACTIVITIES

Playful adult-led activities are adult-led activities that teach children FMS in a playful way, for example passing, throwing and catching a ball. It is important that these activities are non-competitive. Research shows that when activity becomes too competitive it can turn children off engaging in exercise and active play. Remember the golden rule: it's not the product that's important, it's the process!

ACTIVITY IDEAS

Some simple traditional childhood games which are really good for getting children active and engaging in their FMS include the following:

- **Hopscotch:** This helps children to develop balance and locomotor skills as they hop on one leg.
- **Simon Says:** This game helps to develop balance skills as children 'freeze' in different poses.
- **Chase:** This game helps to develop locomotor skills as children run and gallop in an attempt to not be 'caught'.
- **Ball games:** When children throw, catch and kick a ball they are developing their manipulation skills.

Group activity

In groups make a list of the active games you played as children. Then spider diagram which FMS each game would help to develop.

Activity Ideas for Children by Age Group

Physical activity can be encouraged from the first days of a baby's life. As the child grows and gets stronger, they become more active and develop increasing control over their body. The HSE document *Active Play Every Day* has a list of different activity ideas for children at different ages.

0–6 MONTHS

- Babies should have a little tummy time every day. Tummy time is when the baby is placed on their tummy. This allows babies to stretch and develop their muscles.
- Nappy-free time can encourage leg kicking.

- Lie the baby on a baby mat under hanging mobiles. This will encourage them to reach, grasp and kick their legs.
- Guide the baby's hands to play games like Head, Shoulders, Knees and Toes.
- Place toys out of reach to encourage the baby to move and reach.

6–9 MONTHS

* Play games like peek-a-boo and pat-a-cake to encourage movement.
* Play music and hold, rock or dance with the baby in your arms.
* Encourage the baby to crawl/shuffle. Give the baby space to move and place objects out of their reach to encourage them to crawl/shuffle towards them.

9–12 MONTHS

* Sit on the floor and roll a soft ball to the baby.
* Play games that involve movement like picking up, pouring, giving and taking.
* Encourage standing and walking while holding on to sturdy furniture.
* Stand behind the child, holding their two hands to encourage walking.
* Teach climbing up and down from the sofa and stairs.
* Continue action games and songs.

12–18 MONTHS

* Encourage first steps by kneeling in front of the child with your arms open wide.
* Teach the child to walk sideways and backwards while holding their hands.
* Give them a large, wheeled toy to push and pull.
* Encourage them to squat to pick up toys.
* Continue to encourage climbing.
* Let them fill and empty toys from a box or basket.

18–24 MONTHS

* Encourage walking in different directions and on different surfaces.
* Support the child to start walking up steps and stairs.
* Encourage kicking a light ball between you or off a wall.

* Play simple games of chase.
* Blow bubbles for the child to 'catch'.

2–3 YEARS

* Encourage ball activities, such as kicking, catching, throwing.
* Play music and action songs and games, such as Ring a Ring a Rosy.
* Have children help with little jobs around the house or the ELC setting.
* Encourage them to push or pedal a tricycle or other wheeled toys.
* Continue to play chasing games and hide-and-seek.

3–4 YEARS

* Teach movement cues like 'stop' and 'start', as well as 'your turn' with games like Simon Says.
* Play ball games to show children how to bounce, throw and kick a ball. Give children different kinds of balls and balloons to practise their skills.

* Dance and move to music.
* Strengthen muscles and bones through a relaxing and fun activity such as yoga.

4–5 YEARS

* Play Animal Walks – the child acts out different animals and has to imitate their movement.
* Teach batting skills, such as swinging a toy baseball or golf club.
* Teach ball games like soccer or football.
* Encourage risky play for children to push their physical capabilities.

5–6 YEARS

* Play games with instructions, such as What Time Is It, Mr Wolf?
* Create mini-obstacle courses for children to explore their emerging abilities.
* Encourage risky play for children to push their physical capabilities.

Partnership with parents

Parents should be informed that the service will promote active play and physical activity. If a parent has a particular interest in sport or physical activity they could be asked to come in and help out with a sports day, for example. Parents should also understand the importance of risky play for their child and be informed about the ELC setting's risky play policy.

Inclusive Active Play

The Level 5 funding available under the Access and Inclusion Model (AIM) entitles ELC settings to apply for funding to enable children with additional needs to access and meaningfully participate in the ELC setting. This might involve physical works to the building to enable to child to engage in active play, for example installing ramps or purchasing specialised trikes. The ELC setting should facilitate all children to engage in physical activity and risky play, including those with additional needs. All ELC settings have an AIM Inclusive Play (AIP) pack, which includes some toys specially designed for children with additional needs such as soft foam balls, dancing ribbons and tactile balls. These can be used by all children to make active play inclusive for all.

CASE STUDY: INCLUSIVE ACTIVE PLAY

Conor is 3 and attends the ECCE room of Little Treasures Early Years setting. Little Treasures values being outside and active play. Conor is a wheelchair user and has the support of an AIM worker to lower the ratio of children to adults in the ECCE room. Little Treasures applied for funding under AIM and was able to lay down concrete paths to enable Conor to access the outside easily. Conor and all the other children use the AIP pack, which has inclusive toys including:

* a soft foam ball that makes a sound
* tactile balls, which the children can squeeze.

Conor and the other children play with these outside. Little Treasures bought a basketball hoop, which is adjustable in height, that Conor and the other children use in their play. The outside area also has a sandbox that is wheelchair accessible, and Conor makes patterns in the sand using different toys.

On days when it is raining and too wet to go outside, the children have 'music and movement' time. Conor loves to dance using his arms. He loves to swirl the dancing ribbons that came in the AIM Inclusive Play pack and make patterns in the air with them.

REFLECTION

Reflect on how the children in your professional placement setting are given opportunities for active play and risky play. Are there ways that children could be encouraged to engage in more active and risky play?

Glossary

Chronic condition: a long-lasting condition that cannot be cured but can be managed, and which lasts or is expected to last more than three months

Colostrum: the first breastmilk produced by the mother. Colostrum is high in antibodies.

Fundamental movement skills (FMS): the basic physical movements that children need to learn in childhood that set the foundations for activity and exercise in later childhood and adulthood

Harm: The Children First Act 2015 defines harm as assault, ill-treatment or neglect of the child which seriously affects or is likely to seriously affect the child's health, development or welfare. Any sexual abuse of the child is classified as harm under the 2015 act.

Immunisation: the process by which children develop immunity to disease

Key person: the ELC practitioner responsible for the provision of the lead support, contact and communication for an individual child and their family within the ELC setting

Mandated person: As listed in the Children First Act 2015, a mandated person has legal responsibilities to report child protection concerns above a defined threshold to Tusla. ELC practitioners are mandated persons.

Notifiable illness: Certain illnesses are defined as notifiable illness under legislation. This means medical practitioners must notify the Medical Officer of Health or the Director of Public Health of incidents of these illnesses.

Safeguarding: the principles and procedures to be observed in an ELC setting to keep children safe from harm

Signs and symptoms: A sign of illness is easily observable by the adult caring for the child, for example a runny nose. A symptom of illness is not readily observable by the adult, but will be felt by the child, for example a headache.

Sterilising: the process to remove harmful bacteria that a baby's developing immune system cannot yet deal with

Sudden Infant Death Syndrome: the sudden and unexplained death of an infant under 1 year

Transition: the term given to the process of a person moving from one situation to another. It is not considered complete until the person has fully settled in.

Weaning: the term given to the gradual introduction of solid foods into the diet

References

Behan, S., Belton, S., Peers, C., O'Connor, N.E. and Issartel, J. (2019) 'Moving Well – Being Well: Investigating the Maturation of Fundamental Movement Skill Proficiency Across Sex in Irish Children Aged Five to Twelve. In: *Journal of Sports Sciences*, 37(22), pp. 2604–2612.

Bruce, T., Meggitt, C. and Grenier, J. (2016) *Child Care and Education.* London: Hodder Education.

Bunreacht na hÉireann (Constitution of Ireland) (1937). Dublin: Stationery Office.

Casey, M. and Phelan, A. (2008) 'Introducing Bug Busting: An Action Research to Treat and Prevent Head Lice'. Available from www.ichn.ie/uploads/Bug_Busting_An_Action_Research_Study_to_Treat_and_Prevent_Head_Lice.pdf [accessed 14 July 2021].

Childcare Act 1991 (1991) Dublin: Stationery Office.

Childcare Act 1991 (Early Years Services) Regulations 2016. Dublin: Stationery Office.

Children First Act 2015 (2015). Dublin: Stationary Office.

Corapci, F., Calatroni, A., Kaciroti, N., Jimenez, E. and Lozoff, B. (2010) 'Longitudinal Evaluation of Externalizing and Internalizing Behavior Problems Following Iron Deficiency in Infancy. In: *Journal of Paediatric Psychology,* 35(3), pp. 296–305.

Department of Children and Youth Affairs (2018) *Code of Professional Responsibilities and Code of Ethics for Early Years Educators*. Dublin: Stationary Office.

Department of Education and Skills (DES) (2017) *Síolta: The National Quality Framework for Early Childhood Education*. Dublin: DES.

___ (2017) *Children First National Guidance for the Protection Welfare of Children.* Dublin: Stationery Office.

Department of Children Equality, Disability, Integration and Youth (DCEDIY) (2021*) State of the Nation's Children.* Available from https://www.gov.ie/en/publication/916ef-sonc-part-3-childrens-outcomes/ [accessed online 12 April 2021].

Department of Health and Children (DoHC) (2004) *Food and Nutrition Guidelines for Pre-School Services*. Dublin: Health Promotion Unit.

___ (2005) *Breastfeeding in Ireland: A 5 year strategic action plan 2005–2010.* Dublin: Department of Health and Children.

DoHC and Health Service Executive (HSE) (2009) *The National Guidelines on Physical Activity for Ireland*. Dublin: Health Service Executive.

Department of Health (undated) *Healthy Eating for 1–4 year olds*. Available on https://www2.hse.ie/wellbeing/child-health/food-portion-sizes-for-children-aged-1-to-4-years/healthy-eating-for-1-to-4-year-olds.pdf [accessed 20th July 2021].

Elfer, P., Goldschmied, E. and Selleck, D.Y. (2003) *Key Persons in the Early Years,* 2nd edition. London: Routledge.

ESRI, *Growing Up in Ireland.* TCD, 2006. Available from www.growingup.ie [accessed July 2021]

Farrell, C., McAvoy, H., Wilde, J. and Combat Poverty Agency (2008) *Tackling Health Inequalities – An All-Ireland Approach to Social Determinants*. Dublin: Combat Poverty Agency/Institute of Public Health in Ireland.

Graham, I. (2012) *Supporting Children through Transitions in their Early Years.* Dublin: Barnardos.

Hayes, N. and Kernan, M. (2008) *Engaging Young Children: A Nurturing Pedagogy*. Dublin: Gill and Macmillan.

Horan, M. and O'Brien, G. (2008) *Ready for School: A Parent's Guide*. Dublin: Veritas Press.

Health Service Executive (HSE) (2006) *Starting to Spoonfeed Your Baby*. Dublin: HSE.

___ (2012) *Management of Infectious Diseases in Childcare Facilities and Other Childcare Settings*. Dublin: HSE.

___ (2019) 'Breastfeeding myths'. Available from https://www2.hse.ie/wellbeing/child-health/breastfeeding-common-myths.html [accessed 31 March 2021].

___ (undated) 'Active Play Every Day'. Available from https://www.ncn.ie/images/PDFs/3-6_yr_active_play_.pdf [accessed 30 April 2021].

___ (undated) 'Three Week Menu Plan'. Available from https://www.safefood.net/getmedia/b36c08e8-f352-43dc-9253-fda149ffeb64/3-week-menu-plan.pdf [accessed 30 April 2021].

Irish Nutrition & Dietetic Institute 'Food Allergies and Intolerances'. Available from https://www.indi.ie/diseases,-allergies-and-medical-conditions/food-allergy-and-intolerance/383-food-allergies-and-intolerances-factsheet.html [accessed online 18 May 2021].

Irish Water Safety, statistical information. Available from www.iws.ie [accessed online 15 May 2021].

Lozoff, B., Klein, N., Nelson, E., McClish, D., Manuel, M. and Chacon, M.E. (1998) 'Behavior of Infants with Iron Deficiency Anaemia. In: *Child Development,* 69(1), pp. 24–36.

Main, M. and Solomon, J. (1990) 'Procedures for Identifying Infants as Disorganised/Disorientated during the Ainsworth Strange Situation'. In: M.T. Greenberg, D. Cicchetti and E.M. Cummings (eds.), *Attachment in the Preschool Years: Theory, Research and Intervention*. Chicago: University of Chicago Press, pp. 121–160.

Maslow, A. (1954) *Personality and Motivation*. New York: Harper & Row.

Maternity Protection Act 2004 (2004). Dublin: Stationery Office.

McMahon, M. (2021) *The Book of Nutrition*. Birdhill: Boru Press.

McPartland, E. (2020) *The Best Interests of the Child*, 3rd edition. Birdhill: Boru Press.

Mitchell, L., Bel-Serrat, S., Stanley, I., Hegarty, T., McCann, L., Mehegan, J., Murrin, C., Heinen, M. and Kelleher, C. (2020) *The Childhood Obesity Surveillance Initiative (COSI) in the Republic of Ireland – Findings from 2018 and 2019*. Dublin: Health Service Executive.

National Collaborating Centre for Women's and Children's Health (2018) 'Urinary tract Infection in Children Diagnosis, Treatment and Long-term Management', 2nd edition. Available from https://www.nice.org.uk/guidance/cg54/evidence/full-guideline-pdf-196566877 [accessed online 2 June 2021].

National Council for Curriculum and Assessment (NCCA) (2009) *Aistear: The Early Childhood Curriculum Framework.* Dublin: NCCA.

___ (2015) 'Fundamental Movement Skills'. Available from https://www.aistearsiolta.ie/en/play/resources-for-sharing/fundamental-movement-skills-3-6-years-.pdf [accessed online 14 April 2021].

___ (undated) *Aistear Síolta Practice Guide*. Available from https://www.aistearsiolta.ie [accessed 10 April 2021].

National Eczema Association (undated) 'Eczema in Skin of Color'. Available from https://nationaleczema.org/eczema-in-skin-of-color [accessed online 24 June 2021].

Nicholson, A. and O' Malley, G. (2009) *When Your Child Is Sick: What you can do to help*. Dublin: Gill and Macmillan.

Safefood (2019) 'The Cost of a Healthy Food Basket'. Available from https://www.safefood.net/news/2019/low-income-household-grocery-shop [accessed online 30 April 2021].

Safety, Health and Welfare at Work Act 2005 (2005). Dublin: Stationery Office.

Sandseter, E.B.H. (2007) 'Categorizing Risky Play – How Can We Identify Risktaking in Children's Play?'. In: *European Early Child Education Research Journal*, 15(2), pp. 237–252.

Schaffer, H.R. (1977) *Mothering*. Cambridge, MA: Harvard University Press.

Schaffer, H.R. and Emerson, P.E. (1964) 'The Development of Social Attachments in Infancy'. In: *Monographs of the Society for Research in Child Development* , 29(4).

Schaffer, D.R. (2005) *Social and Personality Development*, 5th edition. London: Thomson Learning.

Sports Ireland (2018) *The Children's Sport Participation and Physical Activity Survey*. Dublin: Sport Ireland.

Sylva, K., Melhuish, E., Sammons, P., Siraj-Blatchford, I., Taggart, B., Smees, R. and Morahan, M. (2004) 'The Effective Provision of Pre-school Education (EPPE) project'. In: *Children*, 29(30), p. 31.

Taras, H. (2005) 'Nutrition and Student Performance at School'. In: *Journal of School Health, 75(6)*, pp. 199–213.

The Curiosity Approach (2019) 'Process over the Product'. Available from https://www.thecuriosityapproach.com/blog/process-over-product [accessed 30 May 2021].

Unicef (2019) 'The Impact of Poor Diet on Children's Health'. Available from https://www.unicef.org.uk/press-releases/poor-diets-damaging-childrens-health-warns-unicef [accessed online 15 May 2021].

Walton, J. (2012) 'National Pre-School Nutrition Survey: Summary Report on Food and Nutrient Intakes, Physical Measurements and Barriers to Healthy Eating'. Available from www.iuna. net/wp-content/uploads/2012/06/Summary_Report_National_ PreSchool_ Nutrition_Survey_June_2012.pdf [accessed online 30 March 2021].

Wicklow County Council (undated) 'Nappies'. Available from https://www.wicklow.ie/Living/Services/Environment/Recycling-Waste-Management/Community-Schools/Nappies [accessed online 31 March 2021].

Appendices

Appendix 1: Immunisation Schedule for Children in Ireland (2021)

Age to Vaccinate	Type of Vaccination
At 2 months Free from your GP	**6 in 1 Vaccine** (Diphtheria Tetanus Whooping Cough (Pertussis) Hib (Haemophilus influenzae b) Polio (Inactivated poliomyelitis) Hepatitis B)
	PCV (Pneumococcal Conjugate Vaccine)
	MenB Vaccine (Meningococcal B Vaccine)
	Rotavirus oral vaccine
At 4 months Free from your GP	**6 in 1 Vaccine** (Diphtheria Tetanus Whooping Cough (Pertussis) Hib (Haemophilus influenzae b) Polio (Inactivated poliomyelitis) Hepatitis B)
	MenB Vaccine (Meningococcal B Vaccine)
	Rotavirus oral vaccine
At 6 months Free from your GP	**6 in 1 Vaccine** (Diphtheria Tetanus Whooping Cough (Pertussis) Hib (Haemophilus influenzae b) Polio (Inactivated poliomyelitis) Hepatitis B)
	PCV (Pneumococcal Conjugate Vaccine)
	MenC Vaccine (Meningococcal C Vaccine)
At 12 months Free from your GP	**MMR** (Measles Mumps Rubella)
	MenB Vaccine (Meningococcal B Vaccine)
At 13 months Free from your GP	**Hib/MenC** (Haemophilus influenzae b and Meningococcal C combined vaccine)
	PCV (Pneumococcal Conjugate Vaccine)

(Source: https://www.hse.ie/eng/health/immunisation/pubinfo/pcischedule/immschedule/)

Appendix 2: List of Notifiable Diseases

Notifiable Diseases and their respective causative pathogens
specified to be Infectious Diseases under Infectious Diseases (Amendment) Regulations 2020 (S.I. No. 53 of 2020) February 2020

Disease	Causative Pathogen
Acute anterior poliomyelitis	Polio virus
Ano-genital warts	Human papilloma virus
Anthrax	Bacillus anthracis
Bacillus cereus food-borne infection/intoxication	Bacillus cereus
Bacterial meningitis (not otherwise specified)	
Botulism	Clostridium botulinum
Brucellosis	Brucella spp.
Campylobacter Infection	Campylobacter spp.
Carbapenemase producing *Enterobacteriaceae*, Infection or colonisation	Carbapenemase producing Enterobacteriaceae, infection or colonisation
Chancroid	Haemophilus ducreyi
Chickenpox – hospitalised cases	Varicella-zoster virus
Chikungunya disease	Chikungunya virus
Chlamydia trachomatis Infection (genital)	Chlamydia trachomatis
Cholera	Vibrio cholerae
Clostridium difficile Infection	Clostridium difficile
Clostridium perfringens (type A) food-borne disease	Clostridium perfringens
COVID-19	SARS-CoV-2
Creutzfeldt Jakob disease variant Creutzfeldt Jakob disease	
Cryptosporidiosis	Cryptosporidium parvum, hominis
Cytomegalovirus Infection (congenital)	Cytomegalovirus
Dengue fever	Dengue virus
Diphtheria	Corynebacterium diphtheriae or ulcerans (toxin producing)
Echinococcosis	Echinococcus spp.
Enterococcal bacteraemia	Enterococcus spp. (blood)
Escherichia coli Infection (Invasive)	Escherichia coli (blood, CSF)
Giardiasis	Giardia lamblia
Gonorrhoea	Neisseria gonorrhoeae
Granuloma Inguinale	Klebsiella granulomatis
Haemophilus Influenzae disease (Invasive)	Haemophilus Influenzae (blood, CSF or other normally sterile site)
Hepatitis A (acute) Infection	Hepatitis A virus
Hepatitis B (acute and chronic) Infection	Hepatitis B virus
Hepatitis C Infection	Hepatitis C virus
Hepatitis E Infection	Hepatitis E virus
Herpes simplex (genital)	Herpes simplex virus
Herpes simplex (neonatal)	Herpes simplex virus
Human immunodeficiency virus Infection	Human immunodeficiency virus
Influenza	Influenza A and B virus
Klebsiella pneumoniae Infection (Invasive)	Klebsiella pneumoniae (blood or CSF)
Legionellosis	Legionella spp.
Leprosy	Mycobacterium leprae
Leptospirosis	Leptospira spp.
Listeriosis	Listeria monocytogenes
Lyme disease (neuroborreliosis)	Borrelia burgdorferi
Lymphogranuloma venereum	Chlamydia trachomatis
Malaria	Plasmodium falciparum, vivax, knowlesi, ovale, malariae
mcr-positive *Enterobacteriaceae* Infection or colonisation	mcr-positive Enterobacteriaceae infection or colonisation

Disease	Causative Pathogen
Measles	Measles virus
Meningococcal disease	Neisseria meningitidis
Mumps	Mumps virus
Non-specific urethritis	
Novel or Rare Antimicrobial-resistant Organism (NRAO)	
Norovirial Infection	Norovirus
Paratyphoid	Salmonella Paratyphi
Pertussis	Bordetella pertussis
Plague	Yersinia pestis
Pseudomonas aeruginosa Infection (Invasive)	Pseudomonas aeruginosa (blood or CSF)
Q Fever	Coxiella burnetii
Rabies	Rabies virus
Respiratory syncytial virus Infection	Respiratory syncytial virus
Rotavirus Infection	Rotavirus
Rubella	Rubella virus
Salmonellosis	Salmonella spp. other than S. Typhi and S. Paratyphi
Severe Acute Respiratory Syndrome (SARS)	SARS-associated coronavirus
Shigellosis	Shigella spp.
Smallpox	Variola virus
Staphylococcal food poisoning	Enterotoxigenic Staphylococcus aureus
Staphylococcus aureus bacteraemia	Staphylococcus aureus (blood)
Streptococcus group A Infection (Invasive)	Streptococcus pyogenes (blood, CSF or other normally sterile site)
Streptococcus group B Infection (Invasive)	Streptococcus agalactiae (blood, CSF or other normally sterile site)
Streptococcus pneumoniae Infection (Invasive)	Streptococcus pneumoniae (blood, CSF or other normally sterile site)
Syphilis	Treponema pallidum
Tetanus	Clostridium tetani
Toxoplasmosis	Toxoplasma gondii
Trichinosis	Trichinella spp.
Trichomoniasis	Trichomonas vaginalis
Tuberculosis	Mycobacterium tuberculosis complex
Tularemia	Francisella tularensis
Typhoid	Salmonella Typhi
Typhus	Rickettsia prowazekii
Verotoxigenic *Escherichia coli* Infection	Verotoxin producing Escherichia coli
Viral encephalitis	
Viral haemorrhagic fevers	
Viral meningitis	
West Nile fever	West Nile virus
Yellow fever	Yellow fever virus
Yersiniosis	Yersinia enterocolitica, Yersinia pseudotuberculosis
Zika virus Infection	Zika virus

Please refer to the case definitions for the above diseases. The up-to-date list of diseases and case definitions are available on the HPSC website at www.hpsc.ie/notifiablediseases

APPENDICES

East
Counties Dublin, Kildare and Wicklow
Medical Officer of Health,
Department of Public Health,
Room G29,
Dr Steevens' Hospital,
Dublin 8.
Phone: 01 6352145
Fax: 01 6352103

Midlands
Counties Laois, Offaly, Longford and Westmeath
Medical Officer of Health,
Department of Public Health,
Area Office,
Arden Road,
Tullamore,
Co. Offaly.
Phone: 057 9359891
Fax: 057 9359907

Mid West
Counties Clare, Limerick and North Tipperary
Medical Officer of Health,
Department of Public Health,
Mount Kennett House,
Henry Street,
Limerick.
Phone: 061 483337
Fax: 061 464205

North East
Counties Cavan, Louth, Meath and Monaghan
Medical Officer of Health,
Department of Public Health,
Railway Street,
Navan,
Co. Meath.
Phone: 046 9076412
Fax: 046 9072325

North West
County Donegal
Medical Officer of Health,
Department of Public Health,
Iona House,
Upper Main Street,
Ballyshannon,
Co. Donegal.
Phone: 071 9852900
Fax: 071 9852901

Counties Sligo and Leitrim
Medical Officer of Health,
Department of Public Health,
Bridgewater House,
Rockwood Parade,
Sligo.
Phone: 071 9174750
Fax: 071 9138335

South
County Cork
Medical Officer of Health,
Department of Public Health,
Floor 2,
Block 8,
St Finbarr's Hospital,
Douglas Road,
Cork.
Phone: 021 4927601
Fax: 021 4923257

County Kerry
Medical Officer of Health,
Department of Public Health,
Rathass,
Tralee,
Co. Kerry.
Phone: 066 7184548
Fax: 066 7184542

South East
Counties Carlow, Kilkenny, South Tipperary, Waterford and Wexford
Medical Officer of Health,
Department of Public Health,
Lacken,
Dublin Road,
Kilkenny.
Phone: 056 7784142
Fax: 056 7784599

West
Counties Galway, Mayo and Roscommon
Medical Officer of Health,
Department of Public Health,
Merlin Park Hospital,
Galway.
Phone: 091 775200
Fax: 091 758283

(Source: https://www.hpsc.ie/notifiablediseases/listofnotifiablediseases/List%20of%20Notifiable%20Diseases%20February%202020.pdf)

Appendix 3: Sample Letter Informing Parents of the Outbreak of an Infectious Disease in the Setting

Dear Parent or Guardian,

There has been a case of chickenpox in your child's crèche/pre-school and your child may have been exposed. If your child has not had chickenpox before it is quite likely that they will catch it.

WHAT IS CHICKENPOX?

Chickenpox is a common childhood illness. Fever and cold symptoms are often the first signs of illness and are followed by the appearance of the typical rash. The rash starts as small pink bumps, often around the neck, ears, back and stomach. These develop a little water blister, which in turn becomes yellow and oozy and ultimately crusty as it dries. The rash spreads outwards to the whole body, finally involving the lower arms and legs. People may have only a few spots or may be virtually covered with them. In children it is usually a relatively mild illness, however, occasionally complications develop.

WHY SHOULD I BE CONCERNED ABOUT CHICKENPOX?

Chickenpox can be a devastating infection in people with a seriously weakened immune system (such as patients with leukaemia or following an organ transplant). In adults, chickenpox is a much more significant illness than in children and there is a greater risk of complications developing. Chickenpox in pregnancy can cause severe illness and, if contracted in the early stages of pregnancy, may result in abnormalities in the baby.

WHAT SHOULD I DO NOW?

If your child is normally healthy, chickenpox is likely to be a relatively mild illness and no specific precautions are necessary. Symptoms usually develop 10 to 21 days after exposure. The infected person can spread infection for up to three days before the rash appears and until the last pox is crusted and dry. If your child has a weakened immune system, please contact your doctor and let them know that they may have been exposed.

WHAT SHOULD I DO IF I THINK MY CHILD HAS CHICKENPOX?

If you suspect chickenpox, do not bring the child into a crowded surgery waiting room, as this may only spread the infection further. Contact your doctor to confirm the diagnosis.

Do not use aspirin or any products that contain aspirin to control fever if your child has chickenpox, as this has been associated with the development of a rare but serious disease called Reye's syndrome.

CAN MY CHILD STAY IN CRÈCHE/PRE-SCHOOL?

Many children with chickenpox are too sick to attend pre-school and are more comfortable at home. Children can spread the infection to others as long as they still have any spots that are not crusted and dried. Children with chickenpox or shingles should be excluded from pre-school until scabs are dry. This is usually five to seven days after the appearance of the rash. Children with spots that are crusted and dried can safely attend school.

Thank you for giving this your attention. Your family doctor will be able to answer any further questions that you might have about chickenpox.

Yours sincerely

(Source: HSE, 2012)

Useful Websites

Aistear Síolta Practice Guide

   www.aistearsiolta.ie

Asthma Society of Ireland

   www.asthma.ie

Barnardos

   www.barnardos.ie

Brainwave: the Irish Epilepsy Association

   www.epilepsy.ie

Coeliac Society of Ireland

   www.coeliac.ie

Department of Children, Equality, Disability, Integration and Youth

   https://www.gov.ie/en/organisation/department-of-children-equality-disability-integration-and-youth/

Diabetes Federation of Ireland

   www.diabetes.ie

First Five

   first5.gov.ie

Health Promotion Unit (includes links to downloadable leaflets)

   www.hpu.ie

Health Protection Surveillance Centre

   www.hpsc.ie

Health Service Executive

   www.hse.ie

Irish Nutrition and Dietetic Institution

www.indi.ie

Mo Scéal

ncca.ie/en/early-childhood/mo-scéal

National Childhood Network

www.ncn.ie

National Immunisation Office

www.immunisation.ie

Road Safety Authority

www.rsa.ie

World Health Organisation

www.who.int

Index

Access and Inclusion Model (AIM), 179
accidents, 54–60
active play and physical exercise, 169–80
   activity ideas by age group, 176–9
   for babies, 176–7
   case study, 172
   enriching environment, 174–5
   exercise categories, 172–3
   fundamental movement skills (FMS), 170, 173–4
   inclusive active play, 179–80
   partnership with parents, 179
   role of the ELC practitioner, 171–2
   for toddlers/young children, 177–9
AIM Inclusive Play (AIP) pack, 179
Aistear (NCCA, 2009), 3–6, 24
   exploring and thinking, 5–6
   identity and belonging, 32
   Learning Record Template, 27
   physical care, 93
   well-being, 3–4, 16–17, 160
Aistear Síolta Practice Guide, 29, 34
allergies, 164–5
anaphylaxis, 165
appendicitis, 99, 110–11
asphyxia, 56
assault, 8, 10, 11, 181
asthma, 133, 134–5
attachment theory, 23–5
   attachment in ELC settings, 23–4
   multiple attachments, 23
   reciprocal relationships/interactions, 24–5
attention seeking, 103

autonomy, 20–1
   development of, 81–6

babies
   activity ideas for, 176–7
   bottle-feeding, 143–7
   breastfeeding, 141–3
   carrying, 75
   colic, 147–8
   drinks for babies, 148, 158
   feeding issues, 147–8
   holding a newborn, 75
   illnesses, 109–10
   nappy changing, 77–80
   nutrition for, 140–51
   physical care routines, 76–81
   posseting, 99, 145, 147
   reflux, 148
   SIDS, 74, 91–2
   topping and tailing, 76–7
   vitamin D3 supplement, 143
   weaning, 149–51
   wind/winding, 147
baby slings, 75
bacterial infections, 131–2
bedwetting, 86
behaviour
   changes in, 102
   regressive, 102
Best Interests of the Child, The (McPartland, 2020), 14
black hair, 87
black skin, 87, 117
blood poisoning, 131

INDEX

Book of Nutrition, The (McMahon, 2021), 152
bottle-feeding, 143–7
   bottle feeds, making, 143–4
   formula feed, storage of, 146
   how to bottle-feed, 145
   sterilising feeding equipment, 146–7
breast milk, storage of, 142
breastfeeding, 141–3
   advantages of, 142
   colostrum, 140, 141
   disadvantages of, 143
   long-term health benefits of, 142
   rates in Ireland, 141
   WHO recommendations, 141
bronchiolitis, 109, 110
burns/scalds, 54, 55–6

CE mark, 40, 41
chest x-ray, 132
chickenpox, 50, 124–5
Child Care Act (1991), 38, 106
Child Protection and Welfare Reporting Procedure, 9
Child Safeguarding Statement, 8–9
child-initiated play, 174, 175
childhood illnesses, 95–105, 109–17
   babies and infants, 109–10
   chronic condition, 96
   digestive problems, 110–12
   ear infections, 113–14
   eye infections, 114–15
   infestations, 118–22
   medication, policies on, 107
   notifiable illnesses, 106, 108
   physical signs and symptoms, 97–101
   pyschological signs and symptoms, 102–3
   signs and symptoms, 96, 97–103, 181
   skin conditions, 116–18
   urinary tract infections (UTIs), 115
   see also chronic conditions; immunisation; infection
children with additional needs, 33, 40, 77, 89, 179

Children First: National Guidance for the Protection and Welfare of Children (DCYA, 2017), 10
Children First Act (2015), 8, 9–11, 181
children's rights, 12
'Children's Sport Participation and Physical Activity' study, 173
choking, 54, 56–7
chronic conditions, 96, 133–7
   definition, 133, 181
   intellectual effects, 133
   physical effects, 133
   social and emotional effects, 133
   types of, 133–7
cleaning, 46, 51
coeliac condition, 164, 166
colic, 147–8
colostrum, 140, 141, 181
computerised tomography (CT) scan, 132
concussion, 99
conjunctivitis (pink eye), 50, 114–15
constipation, 110, 111–2
Constitution of Ireland, 12
convulsions, 99
cough, 97
COVID-19, 43, 50
cradle cap, 87
creativity and spirituality, 17
croup, 109
cuts, management of, 51
cystic fibrosis, 133, 164

dehydration, 157–8
Department of Children, Equality, Disability, Integration and Youth (DCEDIY), 9
designated liaison person (DLP), 12
diabetes, 133, 136–7
diarrhoea, 44, 50, 100
dietary requirements, 164
   facilitating, 165–8
   food allergies, 165
   gluten free diet, 166
   Hinduism, 168

Jewish law and kosher foods, 167
lactose intolerance, 166–7
Muslim children, 167
partnership with parents, 167
vegetarian, 168
digestive problems, 110–12
Diversity, Equality and Inclusion Charter and Guidelines for Early Childhood Care and Education (DCYA, 2016), 40
drop-off/collection arrangements, 61–2
drowning, 54, 59

ear infections, 99, 113–14
earache, 101
early learning and care (ELC) environment, 37–42
   challenging/stimulating environment, 40–1
   enriching environment, 39–42
   'family wall', 40
   inclusive environment, 40
   outdoor environments, 41, 42
   risky play, 41
   safe and secure premises, 41–2
   safety standards, 40, 41
   standard of, 39
   see also safe environment
Early Years Services Regulations (2016), 38, 40, 42, 60, 61
   healthy eating policy, 161–2
   immunisations, 103–5
   medication, administration of, 107
   nappy changing/toileting children, 80
   nutritious food, 155
   record keeping, 69
   registering children, 70
   sleep and rest, 90
   staffing, 72
eczema, 117–18, 133
Effective Provision of Pre-school Education (EPPE), 23
Emerson, Peggy, 23
EN71 (EU safety mark), 41

encephalitis, 129
English as an additional language (EAL), 33
environment see early learning and care (ELC) environment
epidemic parotitis (mumps), 128
EpiPen, 165
Erikson, Erik, 81
exploring and thinking, 5–6
eye infection (conjunctivitis), 114–15

falls/cuts, 54, 55
'family wall', 40
febrile convulsions, 99
finger foods, 150
fire drill, 63–4
fire safety, 62–4
fire triangle, 62–4
first aid kit, 66
fluid intake, 157–9
food allergies, 164, 165
food intake
   advertising, effects of, 164
   cooking facilities, 164
   culture, 164
   facilities for cooking, 164
   factors influencing, 163–4
   family income, 164
   family and peer influence, 163–4
   health conditions, 164
   time to cook, 164
Food and Nutrition Guidelines for Pre-School Services, 66
food poisoning, 99, 100, 112
food poverty, 164
food pyramid for children, 152–5
   group 1: wholemeal cereals, breads, potatoes, pasta, rice, 153
   group 2: vegetables, salads, fruit, 154
   group 3: milk, yogurt, cheese, 154
   group 4: meat, poultry, fish, eggs, beans, nuts, 154
   group 5: fats, spreads, oils, 155

INDEX

group 6: foods high in fats, salt, sugar, 155
healthy eating guidelines, 156
food refusal, 162–3
fundamental movement skills (FMS), 170, 173–4, 181
   activity ideas, 175–6
   categories, 174
   child-initiated play, 174, 175
   development of, 174
   enriching environment, 174–5
   playful adult-led activities, 174, 175–6
   risky play, 174, 175
   time, 174, 175

galactosaemia, 164
gastroenteritis (tummy bug), 44, 50, 99, 112
General Data Protection Regulations (GDPR), 71–2
German measles, 130
glands, swollen, 97, 101, 128, 130
GlucoGel, 136
glue ear, 113–14
Growing up in Ireland (2019), 134
growth, delayed, 159

hair, caring for, 87
hand, foot and mouth disease, 50, 125–6
handwashing, 44, 46, 47–9
handwashing products, 49
harm, 10–11, 181
   definition, 8, 10
   grounds for concern, 11
head lice, 118, 120–2
headache, 101
Health Service Executive see HSE
healthy eating guidelines, 156
healthy eating policy, 161–2
hepatitis, 99, 104
Hib/Men C vaccine, 131
high temperature, 98–9
Hinduism, 168

HSE
   '3-Week Menu Plan: A Resource for Pre-schools', 156
   chlorine-based disinfectants, 51
   handwashing technique, 47
   notifiable illnesses, list of, 106
   Schools Immunisation programme, 103–4
hygiene, 43–51
   cuts, management of, 51
   handwashing, 47–9
   implementing hygiene measures, 46–51
   infection, transmission of, 43–5
   pathogens, 43, 44–5
   protective clothing, 51
   regular cleaning, 51
hyperglycaemia, 137
hypoglycaemia, 136–7

ill-treatment, 8, 10, 11, 181
illnesses see childhood illnesses
immunisation, 50, 96, 103–5, 181
   active immunity, 103
   herd immunity, 103
   meningitis, Hib and Men C, 131
   minor reactions, 105
   MMR vaccine, 128, 129, 130
   passive immunity, 103
   programme in Ireland, 103–4
   reactions to, 105
   severe reactions, 105
   TB vaccine (BCG), 132–3
Immunisation Passport, 104
impetigo, 50, 116
infection
   bacterial and viral, 123–33
   chain of, 44–5
   direct contact, 43, 44
   exclusion periods, 50
   faecal-oral transmission, 43, 44
   indirect contact, 43, 44
   pathogens, 43
   transmission of, 43–4

infection control policy and procedure, 107
Infectious Diseases (Amendment) Regulations (2020), 106
infestations, 118–22
influenza, 125
inhalers, 134–5
insulin, 136–7
intellectual curiosity, 17
'Introduction to Children First' (Tusla, e-learning programme), 10
irritable mood, 103
Islam, 167

Judaism, 167

key person, 16, 20, 23, 26–7, 181
key practical tasks
   bottle-feeding, 140, 143–4, 145, 146–7
   childhood illnesses, 109
   drop-off and collection arrangements, 61
   fire drill, 63
   hygiene measures, 43, 46
   mealtimes, 140, 152
   nappy changing, 74, 78
   safe environment, 52–3, 60–1, 63–4
   sterilising feeding equipment, 146–7
   toilet training, 82
Kitemark (UK safety symbol), 40, 41
kosher foods, 167

lactose intolerance, 164, 166–7
Laevers, Ferre, 21–3
lymph nodes, swollen, 101

Malaguzzi, Loris, 39
mandated person, 8, 10, 12, 181
mandated reporting, 10, 12
Maslow's hierarchy of needs, 18–20
   love/belonging, 18, 20
   physiological needs, 18, 19
   safety and security, 18, 19
   self-actualisation, 18, 20
   self-esteem, 18, 20

mealtimes, supporting children during, 162–4
measles, 129
medication, policies on, 107
memory and concentration, 160
meningitis, 50, 99, 131–2
Milton, 146
MMR vaccine, 128, 129, 130
Mo Scéal templates, 34
Montessori, Maria, 39
mumps, 50, 128

nail care, 87
nappies, types of, 77–8
nappy changing, 77–80
nappy rash, 80–1
National Immunisation Office, 104
National Physical Activity Guidelines, 173
National Poisons Bureau, 58
'National Pre-School Nutrition Survey' (Walton, 2012), 160
neglect, 8, 10, 11, 181
notifiable illnesses, 106, 108, 128, 129, 130, 132, 133, 181
nutrition, 139–51
   babies, 140–51
   fluid intake, 157–8
   food intake, factors influencing, 163–4
   food pyramid, 152–5
   food refusal, 162–3
   guidelines for pre-school services, 155–8
   healthy eating guidelines, 156
   healthy eating policy, 161–2
   impact of a poor diet, 159–60
   mealtimes, supporting children during, 162–4
   portion size, 156
   role of the ELC practitioner, 161–4
   special diets, 164
   toddlers and young children, 152–65

obesity, 159–60
oral health, 88–90, 159

outings, 64–8
  adult to child ratio, 65
  case study, 67–8
  children's learning, 65
  communication system, 66
  cost, 67
  first aid, 66
  food and drink, 66
  parental permission, 66
  transport, 66
  weather conditions, 67

pain, 101
pathogens, 43, 44–5
personal protective equipment (PPE), 51, 93
physical care, 73
physical care routines, 13, 74–93
  babies and young children, 76–81
  bedwetting, 86
  hair, caring for, 87
  holding a baby, 75
  nappy changing, 77–80
  nappy rash, 80–1
  oral health, 88–90
  SIDS risk factors, 91–2
  skin, caring for, 87
  sleep and rest, 90
  staff, personal care, 92–3
  toilet training, 82–5
physical well-being, 17
pink eye (conjunctivitis), 114–15
PKU (phenylketonuria), 164
poisoning, 54, 57–8
posseting, 99, 145, 147
premises, safety and security of, 41–2
protective clothing, 51, 93
psychological and social well-being, 17
Public Poisons Information Line, 58

Quality and Regulatory Framework (QRF) (Tusla, 2018), 38, 42, 63, 69

Ramadan, 167
record keeping, 69–72
  case study, 71–2
  confidentiality, 70
  GDPR, 70–1
  informed consent, 70
  registering children, 70
reflux, 148
regressive behaviour, 102
respiratory infection, 99, 142
ringworm, 116
risky play, 174, 175, 178, 179, 180
rubella, 50, 130
runny nose, 98

safe environment, 52–68
  accident and incident policy, 60
  accidents, 54–60
  case study, 59–60
  daily checks, 54
  drop-off/collection arrangements, 61–2
  fire safety, 62–4
  hazards/risks, 54, 55
  legal requirements, 53
  password system, 61
  photo identification, 61
  records of attendance, 61
  signing in and out, 61, 62
safeguarding, 7–14, 181
  Child Safeguarding Statement, 8–9
  confidentiality, responsibilities of, 12
  definition, 8
  physical care routines, 13
  responsibilities in the ELC setting, 13
  rights of children, 12
  rights of the family, 12
Safety, Health and Welfare at Work Act (2005), 57
safety standards marks, 40, 41
scabies, 50, 118, 120
scalds/burns, 54, 55–6
scarlet fever, 50, 126–7

Schaffer, Rudolph, 23
septicaemia, 123, 131
sexual abuse, 8, 10, 11
signing in and out, 61, 62
signs and symptoms of illness, 96, 97–103, 181
   physical, 97–101
   psychological, 102–3
Síolta: the National Quality Framework for Early Childhood Education (DCYA, 2017), 1–2, 24
   Standard 2: Environments, 1, 39, 78
   Standard 3: Parents and Families, 1
   Standard 9: Health and Welfare, 1, 90, 160
   Standard 11: Professional Practice, 2
   Standard 13: Transitions, 2, 29
   Standard 15: Legislation and Regulation, 2
   Standard 16: Community Involvement, 2, 64
skin care, 87
skin conditions, 116–18
slapped cheek, 127
sleep issues, 160
sleep and rest, 90
special diets see dietary requirements
staff, 72
   personal care, 92–3
   safe recruitment, 72
sterilising, 140, 146–7, 181
   boiling method, 147
   chemical sterilisation, 146
   steam sterilisation, 146
strangulation, 54, 57
Sudden Infant Death Syndrome (SIDS), 74, 91–2, 182
   preventing at home, 92
   preventing in the ELC setting, 91–2
   risk factors, 91
suffocation, 54, 57
sunburn, 59
sunstroke, 99
swollen glands, 97, 101, 128, 130

TB (tuberculosis), 50, 132–3
teeth
   caring for, 89–90
   cavities, 159
teething, 88–9
temperature, 98–9
   high, 98–9
   normal, 98
threadworms, 44, 118, 119
toddlers/young children
   activity ideas for, 177–9
   dehydration, 157–8
   drinks for, 158
   fluid intake, 157–8
   food pyramid, 152–5
   food refusal, 162–3
   guidelines for pre-school services, 155–8
   healthy eating guidelines, 156
   impact of a poor diet, 159–60
   nutrition for, 152–65
   portion size, 156
toilet training, 82–5
   accidents, 84
   partnership with parents, 84
   tips, 83–4
   using a potty, 85
   using the toilet, 85
transitions, 28–36, 182
   daily transitions, 29–30
   definition, 28
   ELC setting to primary school, 33–5
   home to ELC setting, 31–3
   major transitions, 29, 31–6
   partnerships with parents, 36
   regular transitions, 29, 30–1
tuberculosis (TB), 50, 132–3
tummy bug, 99, 100, 112
Tusla
   Child Protection and Welfare Report Form, 11
   Early Years Inspectorate, 69, 106, 108, 155

'Introduction to Children First', 10
  reporting to, 10–11, 12

urinary tract infections (UTIs), 86, 109, 115

vegetarian diet, 168
viral infections, 123–31
vitamin D3, 143
vomiting, 50, 99–100

water
  bottle-feeding, 144
  bottled water, 144
  dehydration, 157–8
  functions of, 157
  water softener system, 144
Water Safety Ireland, 59
weaning, 140, 149–51, 182

well-being, 15–27
  Aistear aims of well-being, 3–4, 16–17
  attachment theory, 23–5
  autonomy, development of, 20–1
  case study, 17–18
  creativity and spirituality, 17
  Ferre Laevers scales, 21–3
  intellectual curiosity, 17
  key person approach, 25–7
  Maslow's hierarchy of needs, 18–20
  monitoring/measuring, 21–2
  physical well-being, 17
  psychological and social well-being, 17
whooping cough, 99, 104
wind/winding, 147
World Health Organisation (WHO), 141